LIVING IT DOWN BY LAUGHING IT UP

Living It Down by Laughing It Up

MARTHA BOLTON

SERVANT PUBLICATIONS
ANN ARBOR, MICHIGAN

Vine Books is an imprint of Servant Publications especially designed to
serve evangelical Christians.

All Scripture quotations, unless indicated, are taken from the HOLY
BIBLE, NEW INTERNATIONAL VERSION®. Copyright 1973, 1978, 1984
by International Bible Society. Used by permission of Zondervan
Publishing House. All rights reserved. Verses marked KJV are from the
King James Version.

Published by Servant Publications
P.O. Box 8617
Ann Arbor, Michigan 48107

Cover design: Paz Design Group, Illustrator ?

01 02 03 04 10 9 8 7 6 5 4 3 2 1

Printed in the United States of America
ISBN 1-56955-134-0

LIBRARY OF CONGRESS CATALOGING-IN-PUBLICATION DATA

Bolton, Martha, 1951 -
    Living it down by laughing it up / Martha Bolton.
       p. cm.
    ISBN 1-56955-134-0 (alk. paper)
    1. Faux pas—Juvenile literature. 2. Wit and humor, Juvenile.
    [1. Embarrassment. 2. Wit and humor.] I. Title.

BJ1838 .B65 2001
814'.54—dc21

00-053434

Dedication

This book is dedicated to
Bill and Juanita Hodges ...
good friends, good sports, good people.

Contents

Introduction

He who doesn't laugh at himself leaves the job to others.
— Anonymous

Embarrassing moments. Few of us get through this life without having to endure one or two of them. Or ten or twenty. Or, if you're like me, enough to fill a whole book! Well, maybe not a whole book. Some of my friends have helped me out by generously sharing a few of their own embarrassing experiences. Yes, we've all bared our souls, confessed our blunders down to the very last mortifying detail; we shared so that you might learn. And laugh.

To tell you the truth, we're laughing with you. That's because laughing about our embarrassing moments is the quickest way to start living them down. Laughter nullifies their power. It frees us to see ourselves as we really are—imperfect people. That's healthy. After all, people who think they do no wrong, who believe they've never made a fashion error or said the wrong thing at the wrong time, aren't living in reality. We've all messed up at some time in our lives. We've tripped over words or our feet, we've spilled drinks, knocked over displays, walked out the wrong door setting off the emergency alarm, we've done it all. We readily admit we're not perfect. Oh, we may not be proud of our embarrassing moments. But we're not pretending they didn't happen either. We know these moments have a value. They've taught us how to think a

9

little more before we talk. Or read signs before we open that door that says Do Not Open. We've learned from our blunders and now we're passing along this knowledge to you. Why? Because for some reason when you read about other people's embarrassing situations it makes you feel a whole lot better about your own.

So, stop your blushing. Come out from under those blankets. Take off those sunglasses and start reading and learning from our hundreds of blunders, bloopers, mishaps, mistakes, misspeaks, fashion faux pas, and bad situations that were only made worse when we tried to fix them. We're all human. We goof up, trip over our own feet, laugh out loud at the worst possible times, say the wrong thing at the most inappropriate moment, and unknowingly have varying pieces of our clothing slide to places to which they were never supposed to slide. But we've survived. Every single one of us. "Embarrassment" isn't terminal. I've never heard of its being listed as the cause of death in someone's obituary. No matter how devastating the incident may seem at the time, actually dying from embarrassment isn't something we have to worry about. Sure, we might wish we had a six-foot deep hole to hide in, but we won't die.

Now, sit back, relax, and join us on our journey. You don't have a thing to worry about. These are our embarrassing moments. No one is making you stand up and tell yours. Although we're pretty sure you have them.

For the next few hours, we'll be the ones living down our horrific moments by having a good laugh at ourselves. And hopefully, by the end of this book, you'll be laughing about your embarrassing moments, too.

Chapter 1

SAY WHAT?

The Lord will perfect that which concerneth me.
PSALM 138:8, KJV

Man does not live by words alone, despite the fact that sometimes he has to eat them.

Adlai E. Stevenson

"I can't believe I just said that!"

Words. They can get us into a lot of trouble, can't they? When you think about it, we use thousands upon thousands of words each and every day. We use them at school, at work, at church, on the phone, on the Internet. We scribble them on our notebooks, write them on chalkboards, create with them, quote with them, ask questions with them, answer questions with them, order with them, compliment with them, complain with them, encourage with them, discourage with them, get irritated with them, and love with them. We will no doubt use trillions of words in our lifetime, so it's no wonder we get a few of them mixed up once in a while.

Sometimes we know we've goofed up the minute the words leave our mouths. Other times we don't find out until they've made their way back to us. Which they always do. No matter how far away from them we think we've gotten, our words will always find us. And they often surprise us. We couldn't have said that, we try to convince ourselves. We wouldn't have said that. But more often than not, we did say that. And the only thing we can do at a time like that is to simply make our way up to that all-you-can-eat verbal buffet and start dining on whatever nouns, verbs, or adjectives happened to have gotten us into trouble this time.

We've been at this all our lives. Have you ever watched a baby examining his feet? He inspects his toes, his heels, his ankles, and before long he's got the whole foot in his mouth. You see, the drive to put a foot in our mouth is inherent in human beings, and it shows up in infancy. It's never a very good fit, nor is it beneficial to us in any way, but for some reason we're bound and determined to get that foot in there. We speak before our brain has finished the editing process, saying things we don't mean and using words that make no sense whatsoever. But they're only words. And sometimes the order we put them in can be rather hilarious. So what was that you said again...?

The word genius isn't applicable in football. A genius is a guy like Norman Einstein.

Joe Theisman
NFL Football Quarterback and Sports Analyst

TONGUE-TITHED

When my son, Tony, was asked to say the prayer for the offering one night at church, he was a little nervous. He didn't admit he was, but I think it was obvious when he asked everyone to bow their heads, then proceeded to pray, "Lord, bless us as we bring you our thighs."

INFREQUENT FLYER MILES

Once, while flying to a speaking engagement, I happened to be seated next to a teenager who had never flown before and was a bit apprehensive. I tried to assure her that everything would be all right, and she seemed to calm down a bit. But then, as we began to taxi down the runway, she turned to me and asked, "Do the wings flap when we take off?"

LIFE AND LIMB

"Local Pioneer in Good Health at Time of His Death."
Headline that appeared in a Southern California newspaper following the death of a local citizen

"You should always go to other people's funerals; otherwise, they won't come to yours."

Yogi Berra

"If you're killed, you've lost a very important part of your life."
Brooke Shields

BON APPÉTIT!

One night my son Matt, who was about ten years old at the time, had a friend over for dinner. After we had eaten, all the boys got up from the table, took their dishes over to the sink, and started scraping them off. How sweet, I thought as I walked by. Then I overheard Matt explain to his friend, "If we don't throw it away, she'll serve it to us tomorrow as leftovers."

"The streets are safe in Philadelphia—it's only the people who make them unsafe."

Frank Rizzo
Former Police Chief and Mayor of Philadelphia

"We've got to pause and ask ourselves: How much clean air do we need?"

Lee Iacocca

"I don't think anyone should write his autobiography until after he's dead."

Samuel Goldwyn

"Outside of the killings, [Washington] has one of the lowest crime rates in the country."

Marion Barry, Mayor of Washington, D.C.

"An excessive loss of altitude."

An airplane crash, as described in a government report

WHAT I MEANT TO SAY WAS...

While preaching an especially spirited sermon one hot Sunday morning, our pastor suddenly stopped midsentence and asked, "Would someone open a window and let some of this hot air out of here?!"

14

JUST FOLLOWING DIRECTIONS

Warning on a television remote control:
"Not dishwasher safe."
(*But how else are we supposed to clean up television?*)

Instructions written on a package of airline peanuts:
"Open packet. Eat contents."
(*Apparently, they don't want us to get confused and start pitching them at the stewardesses.*)

Warning on an iron:
"Do not iron clothes on body."
(*Think of all the plastic surgeons you'll be putting out of business.*)

On the back side of a cardboard windshield protector:
"Please remove before driving."
(*Unless driving in Los Angeles, in which case a lack of visibility is usually recommended.*)

On a shipment of hammers:
"May be harmful if swallowed."
(*But I bet it can really clear up an esophagus blockage!*)

"Experience enables you to recognize a mistake when you make it again."

Franklin P. Jones

AREN'T I WORTH A LITTLE MORE THAN THAT?

I recently received an e-mail from Torry Martin, a comedian and good friend, which included a slight typo. Needless to say, when I brought it to his attention he was mortified. This is how it read: "Also, Martha, on another note ... if I end up getting booked at a few places, that means I'll be bringing in some money and I would like to be able to start paying you for all you do, but I need to know what you charge for the kind of help you give me. It's not enough for me to simply appreciate all your help, you need to be constipated too."

CATALINA ANYONE?

After a Bob Hope television special taping at NBC in Burbank, I was standing in the parking lot of the studio talking with one of the other writers. A man in a car drove up to us and asked, "Can you tell me where Catalina is?" I knew the answer and quickly and confidently volunteered it. "It's across the ocean, about twenty-three miles, I think."

Satisfied, I turned back to the other writer, who greeted me with a rather puzzled look. Then, pointing to the street that bordered NBC, he said to the man, "That's Catalina."

All right, so I was new to NBC and didn't know it sat on a street named Catalina. The only Catalina I knew about was the island. The man in the car thanked my friend for the correct directions, gave *me* a strange look, then proceeded on his way. I felt pretty stupid, but I'm happy to say that the street has since been renamed Bob Hope Drive. It's a lot easier to remember, yet I can't help but wonder if it's affected Catalina tourism any.

CLEAN COMEDY

Once when I called a comedian friend to discuss some business, his son answered the telephone.

"Is your dad there?" I asked.

"No," he said.

"Could you take a message for me then?"

He assured me he could, so I proceeded to give him my message while he wrote it down, having me spell several words in the process. Halfway through my message, though, the lad cut me off.

"Wait!" he said, frustrated. "I'm running out of room on the soap!"

I didn't even ask.

HANG-UPS

In today's world, so many of our calls are answered by machines that we've almost come to expect it. I called a place of business in San Francisco a few years ago and was caught off guard when I heard a live person's voice on the other end of the line. So much so that it took me several seconds to answer the greeting.

"Hello?" the voice pressed.

"You're a real person?" I said, surprised.

"Sure am," she said, impatiently. "Want me to hang up on you and prove it?"

Maybe answering machines aren't so bad after all.

AS I WAS SAYING ...

"Keep a stiff upper chin."

Samuel Goldwyn

"I believe we are on an irreversible trend toward more freedom and democracy—but that could change."

Former Vice President Dan Quayle

LA CUCURACHA

A customer at a local fast-food restaurant had noticed a cockroach crawling on the counter by the table where he was seated. Not only did he complain to the manager, but to the town newspaper as well. In the following morning's paper there was an article about the incident, and in it were several quotes by the manager, including this one:

"I knew we had a mouse problem, but I didn't know we had a cockroach problem."

"I get to go to lots of overseas places, like Canada."

Britney Spears
(when asked about the best part of being famous)

"You better cut the pizza in four pieces because I'm not hungry enough to eat six."

Yogi Berra

"I'm not indecisive. Am I indecisive?"

Jim Scheibel
Mayor of St. Paul, Minnesota

"It's wonderful to be here in the great state of Chicago."

Former Vice President Dan Quayle

"We're going to turn this team around 360 degrees."

Jason Kidd
after being drafted to the Dallas Mavericks

"Half this game is 90 percent mental."

Yogi Berra

"There is no reason why anyone would want a computer in their home."

Ken Olson
President, Chairman, and Founder of
Digital Equipment Corporation, 1977

"I didn't really say everything I said."

Yogi Berra

CRITICS ... EVERYBODY HAS THEM

"Thank you for sending me a copy of your book. I'll waste no time reading it."

Moses Hades

"The covers of this book are too far apart."

Ambrose Bierce

"From the moment I picked up your book until I laid it down, I was convulsed with laughter. Someday I intend reading it."

Groucho Marx

ALL OF ME

At a news conference following a well-known sports figure's liver transplant, the doctor explained to the media that the donor had not only donated his liver but also six other vital organs, such as his heart, lungs, pancreas, kidneys, and eyes.

Impressed and no doubt anxious to get an exclusive, one of the reporters asked the doctor, "Is the donor still alive?"

The doctor, surprised at the naiveté of the question and trying his best to stifle his laughter, simply asked, "Are you a sports reporter, sir?"

"Don't be afraid to make a mistake. Your readers might like it."
William Randolph Hearst

TEA, ANYONE?

Rich Swingle, Actor, Writer

I was in England with my one-person play, "A Clear Leading." My tour manager kept promising we'd splurge on a Devon Cream Tea when we got that far south. As it happened, our host family in Plymouth, on the south shore, was planning on making us a proper Devon Cream Tea. I was quite excited about this, and when we returned from setting up the space for the performance, our Cream Tea was prepared.

When I walked in our hostess asked what I would like to drink. "A Devon Cream Tea, of course!" I said, surprised she had asked the question.

"That's the meal," she laughed. "What would you like to drink with it?"

As it turns out, in most places in England, tea is the late

afternoon meal. In fact, she mentioned that her family had crumpets (an integral element of the Devon Cream Tea) "with breakfast, lunch, and tea."

The next morning our hostess commented, "I think it's amazing that you're able to come all the way across the Pond with your costume, props, and all your luggage." My tour manager responded half-jokingly, "It's because he only brings one pair of pants."

"Actually, I brought two," I retorted.

It wasn't until hours later that I remembered the English use the word "pants" to refer to what they wear under their trousers. Luckily, our hostess had spent enough time in America to know that I didn't do laundry every other night ... or worse.

"The only real mistake is the one from which we learn nothing."

John Powell

Chapter 2

IT'S ALL A MISUNDERSTANDING

> *"God is our refuge and strength, an ever-present help in trouble."*
>
> PSALM 46:1

"I have learned throughout my life as a composer chiefly through my mistakes and pursuits of false assumptions, not my exposure to founts of wisdom and knowledge."

Igor Stravinsky

Misunderstandings can cause a lot of embarrassing situations, can't they? Maybe you gave a friend the wrong directions to the game on Friday night and he ended up in Boise instead of Buffalo. Maybe you gave another friend the wrong homework assignment, mixing up the metal shop project with a recipe for home economics class. (Frankly, that's how I get most of my recipes.) Or perhaps your parents told you to "hold" your baby brother and you thought they said to "hose" him and now he's surfing his way through the den.

The funny thing about misunderstandings is that when we try to explain our way out of them, it often just makes matters worse. If you've ever had the occasion to learn this through a firsthand experience, take consolation in the fact that you're not alone.

THAT'S NO EXCUSE

When one of my sons had to stay home from school due to a cold, I absentmindedly sent the following note to the attendance office the next day: "Tony Bolton did not attend school yesterday because he felt well."

HAPPY BIRTHDAY TO ME!

One of the biggest misunderstandings I've ever had to endure happened one night when my husband was working late. We had planned to meet some friends of ours at a restaurant about twenty miles from our house. My husband had a meeting to attend, so I was going to go ahead to the restaurant, where he'd meet us when he was done. Before leaving the house I telephoned his office and left a message that included the pager number of our friends, in case he should need to get in touch with them for any reason.

The meeting ran longer than he had anticipated, so when he received the message, he telephoned our friends to explain that he wouldn't be able to make it to dinner. He figured they'd go on and meet me at the restaurant and we could still have a good time. Our friends thought he was canceling for both of us and went home.

Meanwhile, I was at the restaurant at a table for six. The restaurant was crowded that night and the hostess couldn't resist the temptation to ask, every time she walked by, "Are you sure your party will be joining you?" With all the customers who were waiting, she could have used the extra seating. I had to keep assuring her that my party was indeed coming. To prove my confidence, I even ordered two plates of appetizers.

I figured that would at least give me something to nibble on until everyone arrived, which was sure to be at any minute.

An hour rolled by. I polished off one plate of appetizers and started in on the other one. I watched the parking lot, but there wasn't any sign of the rest of my party. And speaking of party, as if I wasn't embarrassed enough already, I looked up just in time to see a line of waiters and waitresses walking toward me holding a dessert with a lit candle and singing a rousing chorus of "Happy Birthday." Every eye in the restaurant was on the pitiful lady celebrating her birthday all alone at a table for six.

The people at the table next to me, the ones hidden in the corner, unseen by the other patrons, were the ones really celebrating a birthday.

Needless to say, it was a long night. When I finally got up and walked to the pay phone to try calling home, my husband answered and we discovered the mix-up. There wasn't a thing I could do about it at that point, so I simply walked back to the table, polished off that second plate of appetizers, and ordered a steak dinner to go with it. I figured I might as well make the best of a bad situation. After all, it was my "birthday."

WHAT LANGUAGE ARE YOU SPEAKING?

Laura Whidden-Wetterlin, Singer/Songwriter

Ah, the joys of student exchange. After six months in Valencia, Spain, I had become quite confident in my newfound language skills, and just in time for the family to come visit me on spring break. Hugs and kisses to my parents and cousins were followed by a grueling trip down the coast in my father's compact rental car.

A thirty-five-dollar toll and four hours later we arrived at a cozy hotel in southern Spain. Our bellies led us immediately to a restaurant, which was deserted except for a handsome waiter and one loyal patron.

Our waiter, Mr. Spanish Teen 1995, came over to take our order, and I immediately designated my eighteen-year-old self as the ever important translator. Flipping my long blond hair, I began to explain that my mother wanted a salad with avocado and cheese, my father wanted a tortilla sandwich, and so on. The dashing "camerero" immediately complimented me on my Spanish and asked how long I'd been in the country. He was astonished when I explained how short my stay had been.

Thirty minutes later, our food began to arrive, but to my mother's dismay, her much-beloved avocados were absent from the bed of fluffy greens. I signaled for the waiter and began to plan in my head how I would explain my complaint without offending his dark and handsome sensibilities.

I decided on the phrase, "I don't want to complain, but we're missing avocado on the salad." I knew all the words in this sentence except for the pivotal "complain." It was too late, however; the waiter had arrived, so I spit it out, *"No quiero conejar, pero nos falta aguacate en la ensalada."* The features of his dark face twisted first into confusion, then into suppressed mirth, and finally into uncontrolled bouts of laughter. My family sat in blank ignorance, and the other patron looked up from his drink and stared at me in disbelief as I racked my brain, furiously trying to figure out what I'd said. I knew the trouble must have been with the word "complain." Slowly, I realized what I had done. In the Spanish language, to make any word into a verb you simply slap the postscript "ar" onto the end of it—i.e., "work" ("trabajo") is changed to "to work" by making it "trabajar." Unfortunately for me, I had chosen the word "rabbit," thus making my request, "I don't want to rabbit, but we're missing avocado on the salad."

The waiter continued to laugh, and finding only puzzled looks at our table, he went to the other customer and shared the story with him until he began to slosh his drink in uncontrolled laughter as well.

A month later I was at my voice lesson back at school when I repeated the incident to my teacher. I had found the story to be a very effective conversation piece with the Spaniards, as they always laughed an exorbitant amount with each retelling of my faux pas. When I finished, my teacher looked at me in blank astonishment and asked, "Laura, do you know what that means?"

I responded cheerfully, "Of course, conejo ... hop, hop, hop," as I gestured with my hand along the back of the piano.

"Yes, it means rabbit, but, Laura, you made it a verb. What do rabbits do????"

Thus, you have the painfully embarrassing story of how an overconfident exchange student learned the Spanish slang for reproduction, making the actual translation of my request, "I don't want to have your children, but we're missing avocado on the salad."

Que viva España!

MAKES SENSE TO ME

You know those emergency forms the school district has students fill out at the beginning of each new school year? One year when he was in elementary school, my son Matt filled his out and brought it home for me to sign. Luckily, I read it before signing and turning it back in. Next to the question, "What's your blood type?" he had confidently written "Warm."

MIXED MESSAGES

My son Tony once handed me a napkin containing a telephone message that he had taken from Bob Hope. It simply said, "Bob Hope is going to the doctor tomorrow and needs jokes."

I thought this was a bit peculiar, and even though I was a little embarrassed, I telephoned the boss just to double-check. "You want jokes to tell your doctor?" I asked.

"No," he laughed, then corrected the message. "I'm receiving an honorary doctorate tomorrow and I'd like something clever to say. But I do have a physical coming up ... so don't throw anything away."

WHAT SCRIPTURE WAS THAT AGAIN?
Mike Williams, Comedian

After a comedy show in Malibu, California, I stood at the back of the venue and signed CDs and cassettes. My theme for the night had been patience and how we can have confidence to trust God to work out all things for our good. Along with my signature, I added my traditional "Love, Laugh & Live," and also included the verse of the evening, Psalm 37:7 ("Rest in the Lord and wait patiently for him.").

A couple of days later I began to receive weird responses to my website. People thought what I had written was not quite proper, or even downright rude. I had no idea what I had written that could have upset anyone. I questioned those who mailed me, and soon found out.

Apparently, I had written Psalm 38:7 instead of Psalm 37:7.

Psalm 38:7 says, "For my loins are filled with a loathsome disease."
Needless to say, I sent apologies.

"A clever man commits no minor blunders."

Goethe

"Failure is an event. Never a person."

William D. Brown

"Don't let worry kill you off. Let the church help."

Blurb in church bulletin

Chapter 3

FASHION FAUX PAS

> *"Cast all your anxiety on him because he cares for you."*
> 1 PETER 5:7

"If it is a mistake of the head and not the heart, don't worry about it, that's the way we learn."

Earl Warren

We try our best to be fashionable. We read the latest style magazines, watch the fashion report on CNN, and shop at the trendiest stores. We want to look our best. We dream of or buy designer clothing and get the hottest new haircut. A few of us are even sporting hundred dollar shoes. Still, no matter what we do, no matter how hard we try, we each must accept the likelihood that someday we'll make a dreaded fashion faux pas. And we're not talking just any kind of fashion mistake. We're talking the kind that gets written up in books.

CELEBRITY TRAIN

When Mark Lowry's *Mouth in Motion* went gold, Mark held a press conference in Nashville, Tennessee. Since I had written all the parodies for that musical project, Mark invited me to join him for the conference. It was an important event, so I wanted to look my best. In my hotel room there in Nashville, I tried on one outfit after another, but none of them looked right. Running out of time, I finally returned to the one I had put on first, then darted out the door.

As I was walking toward the elevator, I could feel something brushing against the back of my leg, but I was in too much of a hurry to stop and check. The sensation continued as I stepped out of the elevator on the bottom floor and made my way through the lobby, toward the front doors.

When I reached the entrance, I decided that I probably should take the time to check things out before I drove all the way to the press conference. It was probably just a loose string or something, but why take a chance?

When I turned to look behind me, I discovered that it wasn't a loose string brushing against the back of my legs. It wasn't two loose strings. *It was my nightgown!* With all the changing I had done, it had somehow gotten stuck in my belt, and I was now dragging it along behind me like a bridal train!

I was embarrassed, of course, but at least this ended the mystery as to why the desk clerk had asked if I'd gotten enough sleep the night before!

A COMPLETE ENSEMBLE
Torry Martin, Comedian/Actor

Shortly after moving from Washington State to the Los Angeles area to attend college, I decided I needed to go shopping for some new shorts. I was down to only one pair, and everyone knows shorts and a T-shirt are the Southern California uniform. When I happened upon a sidewalk sale and discovered numerous pairs of shorts in my size, I was elated. I grabbed about ten pairs and began trying them on in the dressing room. About five pairs fit, so I took both bundles up to the checkout counter.

"I'd like to buy all of these," I told the clerk as I handed him the stack of shorts that I wanted to buy. "And you can have these," I said, handing him the second stack of shorts, the ones I didn't want.

"You don't want any of these?" he asked, looking over the rejected stack.

"No. Just those five I've picked out," I said.

"You're sure?" he pressed.

"I'm sure," I said, wondering why he was being so pushy. I was buying five pairs of shorts. Wasn't that enough? Was he working on a quota system or something?

"You're really sure these are all you want?" he continued.

"Yes," I said, emphatically. "These are the only ones I want." I could feel the veins in my neck beginning to bulge.

"All right," he said as he began to ring them up. "I just thought you might like to take these," he said, holding up the pair of shorts I had worn into the store. I didn't even have to look down. I knew at that instant I was standing there in my underwear and shirt. I grabbed my shorts and rushed back to the dressing room to finish dressing. California's casual, but not that casual!

"Everything happens to everybody sooner or later if there is time enough."

George Bernard Shaw

GIVING THEM THE SLIP

Dana Hinton, Royal Marketing/Lillenas

When I was pregnant with my daughter, I was a little skinny thing, and all of my maternity clothes just swallowed me, even when I was eight months along. I wore the clothes proudly, though, because I was so happy to be with child. This one particular Sunday, I happened to be at work as a customer service manager for one of the large retail store chains when, after putting a bag into a customer's buggy and signing my approval of her check, I felt something fall. I looked down and there around my ankles was my beautiful lace-trimmed slip. As gracefully as I could, I kicked it aside and prayed that the customer hadn't seen it.

When the customer left and I bent over to pick up the slip, the store manager, who had been watching me over the security camera, came on the intercom and asked the lingerie manager to "please bring a maternity slip, size small, to Customer Service Manager Dana at the front of the store."

I was still blushing about that when the customer I had been waiting on came back into the store with the two safety pins that had been holding up my slip!

WHAT A WAY TO MEET THE NEIGHBORS!

Reggie Taylor, Comedian

Once, while working on a chicken farm, I was out mending one of the barns. After some time, my lower extremities went numb. When I stood up, my legs were like rubber. There were sharp pains running down my back and legs. I then realized I had been kneeling in an ant bed and they were now all over me. I became their picnic! I quickly decided that I needed to get these intruders off of me, so I got the idea that I would run over to my trailer and shower them off. I took off, but while running I had another bright idea! I decided I'd start taking my clothes off as I ran, so that when I arrived at the shower I could just jump right in!

There I was, running across the pasture: cows were watching, ducks were quacking, goats were bleating, and I was taking off ant-covered clothing as fast as I could.

But you know how they say timing is everything? Mine was a little off that day, because I was running slower than I was taking off my clothes. The problem? I was still nowhere near the shower in the privacy of my own home! Instead, I was standing in the middle of the pasture wearing nothing but a smile, my work boots, and my BVDs! The cows were staring in disbelief, the ducks were quackless, and the goats were blushing. As for the neighbors? Well, I think they were preparing to make a little phone call....

COVERING ALL THE BASES

When my parents were celebrating their fiftieth wedding anniversary, my siblings and I planned a celebration for them. They renewed their marriage vows, and we were able to give them the wedding they had never had. Their children and grandchildren served as bridesmaids, ring bearers, flower girls, and so on. My dad wore a tuxedo and my mother wore a pretty white dress.

The ceremony took place at a historic hotel in Fillmore, California, and part of their wedding gift was a two-night stay there. When we came to check them out of the hotel two days later, they were packed and ready to go, but my father was still wearing his tux. (He liked wearing it and no doubt wanted to get the most for our rental money.) My mother was wearing a comfortable casual dress. I was in shorts.

I didn't really think about our varying clothing styles until we stopped at a nearby restaurant for lunch. After the hostess and several of the other customers gave us a perplexed look, I knew I had to try to explain it somehow. "We weren't sure of the dress code."

They still sat us in the back.

IF THE SHOE FITS ...

I once threw a party at my house for the young adults of my church. One of the games I had planned was one I'd made up earlier that day when I'd realized I needed to have a few games for the party. It was called "Guess the Knees." I draped a sheet over our hallway entrance, making sure that it hung about two feet off the ground. Then I instructed my husband and the rest of the men to go to the back bedroom, roll up their pant legs to the knee, and one at a time make their way down the hallway, fashion-show style. The women were to guess which pair of knees belonged to which man.

The game delivered the laughter I had hoped for, but not for the reason I had expected. When each man appeared, he was wearing a pair of my shoes! I couldn't believe it. After all, there were some big, burly guys there. Construction workers, law enforcement officers, and yes, even our pastor, all managed to get their feet into my shoes, and not one of them complained about their pinching his toes. One of the men even managed to get his feet into a pair of skintight boots!

Oh, well, I guess it could have been worse. They could have had to ask for tissue to stuff the toes!

SAVED BY THE BELL
Heidi Saxton, Author and Editor

I once had an English teacher who, whenever he wanted to impress a certain point upon us, would put one foot up on a desk and lunge forward, waving a ruler in the air to punctuate his remarks.

One day someone got out of line. I don't recall the offense, but I certainly remember the teacher's response. His face got all red, and once again he put his foot up on the desk to lecture us properly. It was then we noticed that the inseam of his pants had split. He was wearing white boxers with little red hearts on them. I kid you not.

The entire class (particularly those in the first row) started tittering. He didn't realize why we were laughing, and thought we were merely being insubordinate, which only made him angrier. I will never forget the sight of my English teacher, spittle flying from the corners of his mouth, shouting at the top of his lungs and slamming the ruler on his desk: "What's so FUNNY? (slam) There's nothing FUNNY (slam) about disrespect! You all are going to get DETENTION! (slam, slam)." With every "slam," he lunged forward, sending the rest of us into fresh paroxysms of laughter. Of course, no one had the nerve to tell him why we were laughing ... but when we told our history teacher (in our next class), she must have passed it on.

That was the last time he ever put his foot on a desk.

HOW'S THE WEATHER?

Once while working on a Bob Hope show at NBC, I took my dinner break at a fast-food restaurant across the street and happened to run into our local weatherman there. I had been doing some writing for him, so he invited me to join him. We took a booth and talked about some of his latest projects, the Hope special, and various other topics. When we were done, we walked to our respective cars and got into them. Before backing out of my parking space, I glanced in my rearview mirror, as I always do before backing out, but what I saw was a lot more than parking lot traffic. A big clump of cheddar cheese had somehow managed to adhere itself to my cheek. I'm sure the weatherman saw it, but he didn't say a single word about it throughout the entire meal! Maybe I shouldn't have expected him to. After all, "scattered cheese coverage" wasn't one of his regular forecasts.

KEEPING YOUR CHIN UP IS GOOD, BUT ONCE IN A WHILE IT'S WISE TO LOOK DOWN

Lynn Keesecker

On my first Sunday as music minister for a large church, I was determined to make a good first impression. I carefully chose the suit, shirt, and tie I would wear and made sure my shoes were shined. In the choir room, I rehearsed the sixty-member choir just before we entered the platform for the call to worship.

Everything went just as planned, and the choir sounded fantastic. As they finished the opening anthem, I turned to the congregation and asked them to join us in singing the first hymn. When we finished, the pastor came to the podium, and I took a seat facing the audience. Just as I closed my eyes for the prayer, I noticed a flash of white against my dark suit pants. I opened my eyes again with horror to see that my zipper was unzipped and my white shirttail was exposed to anyone who was watching me on the elevated platform.

While every head was bowed, I quickly zipped up my pants and then fervently prayed that no one had noticed, knowing that the entire congregation would have had to be blind not to have seen this exhibition. It was a humbling beginning to what became a wonderful church music experience.

SNAP, CRACKLE, AND STATIC CLING

Frances Bell Riley, Writer

After battling **static cling** for years and resisting paying the high cost of **static** cling sheets for the dryer, I finally decided to break down and buy a box.

When Saturday morning arrived, I washed a load of my clothes and rushed around the house, trying to get ready for a baby shower luncheon at a local restaurant. With my load of clothes finally dried, I carried it upstairs to my bedroom. When I pulled my polyester slacks from the pile, my blouse came with it. "I forgot a static sheet," I said, annoyed. However, I was running late and had no time to change. With a quick, "Good-bye kids," I dashed to my car and drove off.

Slightly out of breath, I entered the restaurant and asked the waitress the location of the banquet room. I thanked her and swiftly walked to the far end of the dining area. I had just handed the hostess the gift when a waitress walked over to me, saying, "Ah, I think you dropped something."

"Oh, what?" I asked.

"Mmm, ah ... that," she answered, then pointed to a trail of socks, underpants, and various other unmentionables strewn across the restaurant floor.

"Mine?" I gasped, turning beet red.

"They came from your pant leg," she said. I looked down and saw a sock peeking from my pant cuff. "Don't you use static sheets?" the hostess asked.

I whizzed through the restaurant, picking up my laundry and shoving the items in my purse, keeping my eyes downcast. After everything was collected, I walked directly to the bathroom and into a stall. Removing my slacks, I discovered a pair of knee-high stockings and another pair of underwear clinging to the inside. I slipped my slacks back on, zipped my bulging purse closed, counted to ten, then left to face the public once again.

The next time I dried my clothes, I remembered the static cling sheet.

FASHION TIPS
Brittany Scheiner

Last year at the Christian school I used to attend, all the girls had to wear dresses. I wore nylons a lot, but they were always falling down. Not down to my ankles or anything, but far enough that I always had to pull them up.

One of my teachers once told me that if I wore another pair of underwear over them they would stay up better. I tried this and it worked, so I kept doing it. That is, until one day when the elastic broke in the outer pair. I could feel them inching down with every step I took.

As I was walking into my last class for the day, I realized they were showing a little bit. I've always been known as a bit of an overexaggerator and a loud mouth, and I started screaming.

We had a substitute teacher that day, and she started freaking out because she thought something was really wrong with me. I finally stopped screaming just long enough to tell her what had happened, and then started right back up again. If I had moved, people would have been able to see the underwear even more clearly, so I just stood there while my friends around me tried not to laugh. The teacher told me to quit screaming because it was drawing more attention to the situation. There was another door right behind me that no one was supposed to use, so I didn't think about anyone possibly walking in, but wouldn't you know someone would? And the worst part was, it was the guy I had liked since third grade.

Finally, the teacher got all the girls to line up around me and all the boys to turn around, and I lifted my dress and pulled the extra pair of underwear back up. I have learned never to take clothing tips from that teacher again!

WALK A MILE IN MY SHOES

While standing with a group of ladies in a restaurant lobby one afternoon, one of the women happened to notice another's new shoes.

"How darling!" she oozed. "Where did you get them?"

The other lady answered, then returned the compliment.

"I love your shoes, too!" she beamed. "They're new, aren't they?"

"Yes, I just got them," the first lady bubbled.

Then, as if they were feeling bad for not having complimented my shoes, they both looked down and began, "And your shoes...." That's as far as they got, stopping just short of any praise. I suppose the sight of my, well, how shall I put it, comfortable, but out of style brown shoes caught them a little off guard. All they could get out was, "And your shoes ... are shoes."

"The soul that is within me, no man can degrade."

Frederick Douglas

Chapter 4

OOOOOOPS!

> "Therefore do not worry about tomorrow, for tomorrow will worry about itself. Each day has enough trouble of its own."
>
> MATTHEW 6:34

"Creativity is allowing oneself to make mistakes. Art is knowing which ones to keep."

Scott Adams

Sometimes our embarrassing moments come from being in situations where we make mistakes. These mistakes can be small, medium, or large, and some of us even feel the need to super-size them.

There may be many reasons for these mistakes, including poor judgment, failure to think through to the consequences of our actions, ignorance, naiveté, carelessness, stubbornness, pride, shyness, and a host of others. Whatever the reason, the simple fact is, we blew it. There was the right way to do or say something, and we happened to choose, well, a different way ...

WHAT A GUY!

Dr. Stan Toler, Pastor, Author, Speaker

After building a great introduction to my message on the Ethiopian eunuch, I strayed from the text and said: "He was a servant of the court and served as treasurer ... and no doubt he was a good husband and father for his family!"

AVON CALLING?

Before deciding to move to Nashville, I made a trip there, both on business and to check out the available housing. My husband and I had been looking for a place to move ever since the last level 6.8 California earthquake. (I was tired of my office having a busier travel schedule than I did.)

Mark Lowry had been urging us to move to Nashville for some time, so I decided it was time to fly out and see the Volunteer State for myself.

One day after we had done some work together, Mark gave me a tour of the available housing in and around Nashville, then we went on a visiting tour of several of his friends' homes. One such friend was Buddy Green. Buddy had just moved to a new house, and Mark was pretty sure he'd be able to find his new home from memory. After making several trips around the sub-division where he seemed to think it was, Mark finally spotted it.

"There it is!" he said, pulling into the driveway. He had barely shifted to "Park" when he leaped out of the car excitedly and sprinted toward the open garage.

I followed him into the garage and through the side door, but held back a few steps as Mark walked right on into the house.

I heard a man inside greet Mark with a surprised yelp. It

wasn't Buddy. We were soon to discover that Mark had just walked right into the living room of a total stranger's home!

Mark visited with the man a bit, then asked if he knew where Buddy Green lived. The man said he thought it was on a street about a block away. We apologized for barging into his house (even Jehovah's Witnesses at least knock), and then politely made our exit.

FREE REFILLS, ANYONE?

"Shannon," Student

My most embarrassing moment occurred while at the wedding of a family friend. The reception was held in a fancy ballroom, with a lot of people in attendance. I sat at a table with my mom, dad, grandma, and grandpa. It just so happened that my seat was positioned so that I had to turn around to look up at the front of the room. When we bowed our heads for prayer, I started to turn my body, but suddenly my foot got caught in the tablecloth. All of the glass cups on our table, filled with water, fell over! The tablecloth was soaked, and some of the glasses even broke! Everyone looked up after the prayer was over. I was so embarrassed I could have cried, but I figured the tablecloth was wet enough already!

BY THE DAWN'S EARLY LIGHT

A policeman I know shares the story of the night he and his partner were working the graveyard shift and could barely stay awake. They decided to find an out-of-the-way place and take a little catnap, keeping their radio on at all times, of course, just in case an emergency call came through.

After driving around for a few miles, they happened to notice a dirt road which led to a cluster of large trees. Figuring that'd be the perfect place for them to rest their eyelids for a few minutes, they turned onto the road and parked under the trees. Unfortunately, though, they fell asleep.

As the sun rose the next morning, they could hear voices around them. They opened their eyes, but quickly wished they hadn't. Apparently, in the dark they hadn't noticed that the "secluded area" they'd found to nap in was a public park. Their black-and-white patrol car was parked in the middle of a now very busy city park!

I'm not saying they did a Code 6 (red lights and siren) out of there, but they did burn some rubber across those baseball diamonds!

---

em-bar-rass: verb 1. to make feel uncomfortable or self-conscious

(from Webster's New World Dictionary)

THAT SINKING FEELING
Addie Bales, Student

My most embarrassing moment was when I was in first grade. Every day I would ride home on the bus and it would drop me off a block from my house. I should probably tell you that in my town it rains a lot so there are many storm drains. On this particular day I got off the bus, and as I was waiting for the driver to give us permission to cross, I stepped off the curb onto (hopefully) the storm drain. Little did I know that the drain cover had fallen inside itself, and I fell into the drain about a foot and a half. I got all wet and dirty, and my cries for help caught the driver's attention. She rushed off the bus and fished me out of the drain and drove me home. I cried all the way. Since that incident, I always check to make sure there's a cover on storm drains, so in effect I "look before I leap."

OH, WAITER...

Lieutenant Dan Keef, Los Angeles Police Department

While dining with some friends, the waiter served my salad and I reached for the Italian dressing in the container nearby.

Pouring on a generous portion, I began to eat. About halfway through the salad, however, I noticed something strange. The waiter was beginning to light those containers of dressing. Why was he doing a thing like that, I wondered. Then it dawned on me. My "Italian salad dressing" was kerosene!

... Next time, I'm sticking with bleu cheese!

"Only those who dare to fail greatly can ever achieve greatly."

Robert Francis Kennedy

A CORRECTION IN THE MEDFORD, OREGON, MAIL TRIBUNE

"The grand-prize winner of the dance contest will fly to Reno as a regular passenger—not air freight as stated in last week's ad."

Not very long after getting my driver's license, I had my first roadside problem—I ran out of gas. I guess I was absent in driver's education class the day they covered the importance of reading a gas gauge.

I walked to a nearby filling station and bought a couple of gallons of fuel, and when I returned to my car, I did what I'd seen gas station attendants do every time my parents pulled up to a pump. I lifted the hood of the car and took off the radiator cap. (This was, of course, back in the days when gas station attendants actually lifted your hood.)

A man happened to be driving by and saw me tilting the gasoline can above the radiator. He slammed on his brakes and jumped out of his car, screaming, "What are you doing, lady?!"

"I ran out of gas," I said, wondering what he was so panicked about.

"You don't put it in there," he said, grabbing the can from my hands. "That's the radiator!"

Apparently, all those attendants I had seen lifting the hood of our car had been putting water in the radiator, not gas. The gas went, well, you know, somewhere else.

ATTENTION PLEASE

I was sitting in a church service once when the pastor opened his sermon with, "I want to speak to those of you who perhaps are here this morning."

YOU'VE GOT MAIL

Brio Reader

I once wrote a sweet, mushy e-mail to my boyfriend and accidentally e-mailed it to his parents instead! Yes, they got a laugh out of that one.

FREE AT LAST

Jenny Testerman

The day was October 2, 1996. It was a hectic time for my family. We were not only preparing for my upcoming wedding, which was just ten short days away, but also preparing to lay my father to rest. Any comic relief would have been heaven-sent, but little did we know my dad was about to get the last laugh.

My father was a Vietnam veteran who had retired from service in the Army after more than twenty-five years. He was forty-eight years old and suffered from Post-Traumatic Stress Disorder, in addition to several other ailments, which resulted in many visits to police stations and hospitals, and multiple late-night drives around towns to find him. In fact, the local state-funded psychiatric hospital had refused to ever admit him again, due to the fact that they couldn't take responsibility for tracking him down each time he somehow escaped their lockdown facility.

Whenever the staff would call to tell my stepmother and me about Dad's escapes, we'd privately chuckle that "with all of his training he could probably get out of anything." To the funeral home's embarrassment, that's exactly what he did.

As my father's body was being taken from the hospital to

the funeral home for final preparations, he ... well, this is how they explained it to me:

"It seems every safety system in the hearse failed," said the director.

"What do you mean?" we asked.

"I mean the electromagnets holding your loved one's body in the hearse failed. He went rolling down the road and was hit by a car. We are doing our best to keep the story out of the local paper, and are prepared to do whatever we can to make amends," stated the director.

Unfortunately, part of the story had already hit the local radio station. It seems that earlier that morning, a pair of local deejays had received a call from a telephone lineman. He had witnessed a body fall out of a hearse and start rolling down the street on a gurney. He climbed down from a telephone pole in order to stop it, but not before it was hit by a car. According to the lineman, my dad rolled at least five hundred yards before he could catch up to him.

Several friends had heard about the incident on the radio and told us about it at the viewing, outside the earshot of the embarrassed funeral home director, of course. After the shock of the situation wore off, we all chuckled, picturing my father looking down, smiling from ear to ear over the commotion he was causing and the freedom he at long last had.

"The human race has one really effective weapon, and that is laughter."

Mark Twain

"Victory goes to the player who makes the next-to-last mistake."
Chessmaster Savielly Grigorievitch Tartakower

Chapter 5

HUMBLING EXPERIENCES

"You are my hiding place ..."

PSALM 32:7

"Don't be so humble. You're not that great."

Golda Meir

So why do we have embarrassing moments, anyway? Why do we have to endure blemish eruptions on picture day, or speeches where our tongue seems to take on a mind of its own, or days when all that's left of our dignity is the dig part because that's the only way to make a hole big enough for us to crawl into? Why do we accidentally lean against emergency doors in restaurants, setting off the alarm, or glance in the mirror after an encounter with that cute boy or girl only to discover there's more spinach between our teeth than Popeye saw in his entire career? Who knows? What we do know is this—these kinds of experiences sure have a way of keeping us humble.

DO YOU HAVE ANY I.D.?

Gene Perret, Three-Time Emmy-Winning Comedy Writer

I used to cash a $150 check from Phyllis Diller each week. I'd cash it on Friday when I'd deposit my salary from General Electric. I was always popping my buttons just waiting for the tellers to notice the famous name on the check. One Friday, the teller finally noticed and said, "Hey, Phyllis Diller." I humbly nodded "Yes."

She took the check and showed it to the adjacent tellers. I got even more humble. My hat size, though, got four or five sizes larger. Then, the teller came back to me and asked, "Is she anything like the real Phyllis Diller?" The hat size shrank alarmingly. I said, "That *is* the real Phyllis Diller."

The teller held the check up as if she were inspecting a counterfeit bill. She gazed at it, placed it on the counter, then said dogmatically, "No, it's not."

IT ALL COMES OUT IN THE WASH

A few years ago, I was scheduled to speak at a convention in Branson, Missouri. There were several other speakers on the program, including gifted writer and friend Angela Hunt. The organization booked us in a nice hotel, which just so happened to have really great bathtubs. Bathtubs that had obviously impressed Angela. I know this because on the night we were both to speak, I entered the banquet hall and heard Angela call out to me from across the crowded room, "Martha! Did you take a bath?!"

I've been asked that before at banquets, but usually, people just pass me a note.

WHAT'D YOU SPRAY?

Rev. Cecil Barham

One of my most embarrassing moments came in the early years of my ministry. I was newly married and living in San Antonio, Texas. An invitation came for me to preach at a small church that was meeting in a converted house in a very rural area. It was Sunday night, the small building was full, and the "preach" was flowing.

Toward the closing of my message I walked down to the front of the congregation to make my final climaxing point and was waxing very seriously as well as loudly eloquent when a little boy sitting in the front row with his mother hollered out so that all could hear: "Momma, that man just spit on me!"

That brought both my eloquent moment and my sermon to a speedy close.

JUST FILL IN THE BLANKS

While visiting a beloved ninety-five-year-old aunt in Arkansas one evening, I had the opportunity to read an interview with her that had recently been featured in the local newspaper. One of the questions she was asked was "Who's your favorite author?"

I was both flattered and touched that she had named me.

"I'm your favorite author?" I asked, blushing.

"Aw," she quipped, with a playful twinkle in her eye. "I had to say something!"

NO AUTOGRAPHS, PLEASE

When my very first book was released, I was invited to auto-graph copies of it at the Christian Booksellers Convention. This is an annual event attended by bookstore owners world-wide, and it's where many store owners purchase the bulk of their merchandise for the coming year.

I was excited about the new book and the opportunity to autograph copies, but I have to admit I was a little apprehen-sive (most authors are) about how many people would actually show up. Or not show up.

When I looked at the roster to see who was signing at the same time I was, my fears only increased. I was going to be autographing books at the same time as Carmen, Jerry Falwell, and Kenneth Taylor.

I'm not saying how many people were in my line, but I was signing my autographs in calligraphy!

The only good thing was that my autograph line was near the snack bar and restrooms, and since there were long lines in front of each of those, I figured if my husband angled the camera just right ...

"They stayed away in droves."

Samuel Goldwyn

A HARD DAY'S PHOTO SHOOT

Mac Nelson, Freelance Actor/Director

In 1978 I had just recently appeared as Paul McCartney in a movie called *I Wanna Hold Your Hand* when I received a call from the Don Smythe* Look-a-Like Agency, asking me to come in for an interview. I went to the agency's Sunset

*Name has been changed. 54

Boulevard office and was greeted by a secretary. She informed me that Don had gone out of town and that she would do the interview. Several days later, Don himself called to say he'd like me to be his official Paul McCartney look-alike. "Without ever seeing me in person?" I questioned. I had played the role of Paul in the film, but passing myself off as a look-alike was a different story. He assured me that his secretary's word concerning my close resemblance to Mr. McCartney was enough.

Over a year passed before I heard from them again. Then, one hot summer afternoon the phone rang and a photographer informed me that I was one of about fifteen clients from the agency chosen for a photo shoot for a major magazine. I was to be at the agency office the next day in my Nehru suit.

When I entered the office, there on the sofa sat Marilyn Monroe. I sat down and introduced myself. "Hi, I'm Mac Nelson." She extended her hand. "Hello, I'm Marilyn Monroe. Who is Mac Nelson?"

"I'm Mac," I repeated.

"I don't recall who he is," she whispered in traditional Monroe voice, complete with quivering lips. Realizing her confusion, I laughed and clarified that my real name was Mac Nelson and that my look-alike counterpart was Paul McCartney. At this, she stared directly into my eyes, paused, and hesitantly said, "Yes, I guess you do favor Paul a little."

Within the next five minutes, look-alikes for John Wayne, Sammy Davis Jr., Robert Redford, Jimmy Carter, W.C. Fields, Shirley Temple, Marie Osmond, and a man in a Sherlock Holmes costume all arrived. Mr. Smythe soon appeared from his office door and spoke briefly to about six of his clients before stepping in my direction. When he did, a puzzled look came over his face. Staring at me for what seemed an eternity, he quietly asked, "Who are you?"

"I'm Mac Nelson, your Paul McCartney," I answered. He looked me over thoroughly before he spoke. "Well, I guess you do sorta look like him." Just then Gerald Ford arrived, and Don told us all to follow him downstairs for the photo shoot in the Bank of America parking lot across the street. California tourists dream of driving through Hollywood and seeing just one famous person on the street. Suddenly, motorists found themselves feasting their eyes upon fourteen of the most well-known people in the world, several of whom were supposed to be dead, crossing Sunset Boulevard!

When we reached the bank, we quickly made our way to the parking lot, where the photographer carefully placed us. The camera had clicked only once when Mr. Smythe yelled, "Hold it. Sherlock and McCartney, you can go home. It's not working." Embarrassed, the two of us quietly retraced our steps to the agency and our waiting cars.

As I drove back toward Burbank in the rush hour traffic, I found myself getting angry. This never would have happened had the agent met me ahead of time. We had wasted each other's time. I was so busy preparing the speech I was going to give that agency owner the next day that I don't even remember pulling into Dale's Market, as I did every Thursday, to buy *Drama-logue* magazine.

Picking up the paper, I stood in the long line for the checkout counter. My preoccupation with the events of the day was suddenly interrupted, however, as a lady in front of me looked straight at me and said, "Has anyone ever told you that you look like Paul McCartney?" All I could do was laugh.

I WANNA THANK ...

After receiving a Dove Award nomination for a children's musical that I wrote along with Dennis Allen, I excitedly telephoned a handful of friends to tell them. One friend was my former pastor's wife. She was almost as excited as I was, but apparently didn't quite understand the significance of the award. She brought me back down to earth in a hurry when she ever-so-sincerely asked, "So what do they give the Dumb Award for?"

OLYMPIC TRYOUTS

Kim Messer, Product Development Manager
Lillenas Drama Resources

When I was in college, a group of friends and I decided to go ice skating one night. Most of us were pretty skilled in the sport, but an acting buddy and I considered ourselves a level above the average. All night we skated fast, showing off, and even trying some spins and a few pairs moves, as if we were the next Olympic hopefuls.

Near the end of the evening we got especially adventurous. I saw my friend (I should reveal his name for what he did to me, but I will refrain) skating toward me and setting up for a pairs spin similar to those we had already been doing that night. This time, though, the speed looked a little more intense, and I felt my stomach do a little flip as I tried to brace myself for what was to come.

Suddenly he was there. He grabbed me and tried to turn, and in a second I knew something was horribly wrong. We weren't really going anywhere. Then my legs began to give, my body lurched backward, and I lost control. Pinned down by my partner, I started tearfully laughing as he tried his best to somehow get up gracefully.

That's when I noticed my right leg was behind me, and not at all in a place it normally belongs. I finally felt a warm numbness around my right ankle. Even though I had never broken a bone before in my life, I knew immediately that my ankle had been.

With our concerned friends looming around us, I saw the skating rink staff sending an office chair over to wheel me off the ice.

My hopes for skating in the Olympics were dashed, but then, I thought, there's always snow skiing ...

SNOW SHOW
Cory Wetterlin, Actor, Scriptwriter, and Speaker

The air was cool as it blew through the mousse-plastered hair that hung over his favorite bandana. He matched from head to toe in his highlighter blue, pink, and yellow. Even his skis and poles glowed with fluorescent accents. Yes, this was his day and no one, no challenge, could take it away from him, as the sweet sounds of power rock poured through his earphones.

He had already taken his first couple of runs for the day. Seventeen years old and flawless, his edges cut into the feather-light powder, his skis were as one, and his eyes behind dark sunglasses shed no tear in spite of the cold. He dropped into his next run with the beginning of one of Eddie Van Halen's greatest guitar solos. He sailed down the mountain with ease, soared off even the smallest bump, and slid to the smoothest of stops.

And then ... the challenge. It came from one of the admiring amateurs. A simple jump at the bottom of the main run, under the chairlift. Of course, he could not turn such a thing down; he didn't want to disappoint the fans.

So he mounted the chairlift and ascended the slope. He chose his path down the field of moguls, under the watchful eyes of the gaggle of groupies. Then, like a shot of lightning he leapt from the top of the run and pushed on toward his goal. Reaching the approach track for the jump, he stopped to scout out his attack, then plunged into the trough.

Holding nothing back, he locked his skis into a parallel formation and plummeted toward the approaching drop. As he came to the edge of the precipice, he expected to sail, but suddenly realized he was no longer skiing forward. The front of his skis dropped straight down, plunged into the snow, and stuck straight up, making a large X in the middle of the run.

But his youthful body did not stop at all. Instead, his entire form continued at breakneck speed. He skidded across the snow, his face like a glowing fluorescent hockey puck struck by a massive slap shot. After a few moments he peeled his mangled frame out of the snowbank he had created and took the now lensless goggles off of his face. He didn't even look back to see the laughing faces of his former fan club or the riders on the chairlift above. Piece by piece, he collected his scattered gear and wounded pride. He adjusted his bandana and went straight to the lodge to clean the snow from his ears.

And thus at the tender age of seventeen, I, Cory Wetterlin, learned the true meaning of the age-old proverb, "Pride goeth before a (very, very large, embarrassing, and frigid) fall."

"Be nice to people on your way up because you're going to meet them on your way down."

Jimmy Durante

When I was in high school, one of my favorite sports was touch football. I don't know how good I was at it, but I always tried to give it my all. Like the time I ran some forty yards for a touchdown, but couldn't stop running after I crossed over the end zone. I could see the chain-link fence in front of me and, knowing it wasn't about to move, I decided to break my speed by jumping about three feet into the air before hitting it. It would have been a pretty impressive move, except for the fact that my right foot got stuck in the chain link. When I lowered my body to the ground, my right foot didn't come with it. My teammates were cheering the touchdown, and I tried to act as though nothing was wrong while attempting in vain to maneuver my foot loose from its yard-high captivity.

Finally, the teacher realized my predicament and motioned for several other students to come and help me free myself.

Kinda took the glory out of the moment.

"The secret of how to live without resentment or embarrassment in a world in which I was different from everyone else was to be indifferent to that difference."

Al Capp, Cartoonist

A JOYFUL NOISE

After years of wanting to be able to sing in the choir, I finally got up the courage to attend one of the practices. The director tried me out in the front row, and after lip-syncing my way through the first couple of songs, I finally started to sing. Not just sing, though. I was really belting it out. I was the next

Celine Dion. The new Sandi Patty. The choir director kept giving me looks, and with each glance in my direction, I beamed with pride. She no doubt had never heard a voice like mine. I was the answer to her choir-directing prayers. After two numbers, she couldn't contain herself any longer. She called out my name and I awaited her praise. I was sure she was going to ask why I hadn't joined the choir months ago! But she didn't. "You really have a bad cold, don't you?" she asked, in front of everyone. I didn't have a cold. But my pride was sure starting to feel under the weather.

Oh, well ... she still let me sing in the choir, but I had to face the opposite direction.

DRIVEN TO EMBARRASSMENT

When noted science fiction writer Ray Bradbury agreed to speak at the Simi Valley branch of the National League of American Pen Women's annual writers' dinner, my husband and I were assigned to pick him up for the event. We figured our car wasn't good enough for the job (it had been stalling out on speed bumps), so we borrowed a friend's brand new Cadillac.

Everything went well on the way to Mr. Bradbury's Los Angeles home, but once he got in our car (rather, our friend's car), it began to rain. The windows started to fog up, and my husband tried turning on the defroster. Not being familiar with all the buttons on the dashboard and steering wheel, he ended up turning on everything *except* the defroster. This included the radio, the tape player, the cruise control, the air conditioner, the heater, and the sun roof (this one, of course, was perfectly timed with a cloudburst). I'm not sure what Ray Bradbury thought, but I'm sure he wasn't expecting to have his suit washed and dried before arriving at the banquet.

Then, when we had to stop for gas, we couldn't find where they'd hidden the gas tank and had to ask the gas station attendant to find it for us.

I learned a good lesson that night about pretending to be something you're not. I even wrote about the incident in my newspaper column, confessing that the Cadillac wasn't our car, and sent Ray Bradbury a copy.

From his kind response, it was clear that he'd gotten a good laugh out of the evening himself. He said he enjoyed the ride with us, and even sent me an autographed picture of himself ... inscribed to "Mary." Serves me right, I suppose.

"If a man does his best, what else is there?"

General George S. Patton

Chapter 6

BUT, SERIOUSLY...

> In all these things we are more than conquerors through
> him who loved us.
>
> ROMANS 8:37

"Once we accept our limits, we go beyond them."

Brendan Francis

Life. It's long been said that it's too important to be taken
seriously. That's true. If we can't bend with our blunders and
flow with our foul-ups, we're not going to have a very good
time, are we? We're going to lie in bed at night, replaying
those embarrassing moments over and over in our heads.
We're going to toss and turn knowing we were the one in band
who accidentally washed the brass instruments with soap, and
now all those bubbles on the football field during halftime are
our fault. We're going to fall into the trap of thinking that our
embarrassing moments define who we are. But the only thing
they truly define is the extent of our ability to laugh at ourselves. And that speaks volumes.

GOING TO THE CHAPEL

Wedding bloopers are great. Not only because they're usually done before a live audience, but because they're often caught on videotape, too. Like the wedding I attended where the minister was coming to the close of the ceremony and asked the groom to "take the ring and place it on the third hand of his bride's left finger."

HOW MUCH DO I TIP FOR THIS?
Diane McClay, Royal Marketing

Our office goes to an international convention out of town once a year. We rent a van and go out to very nice restaurants for dinner together. These vans have several rows of rear seats. The first one usually has a portion of the seat that folds down and out of the way to allow the people in the far backseat to walk out.

That seat in our van was broken and not folding down, so my friend and I decided we'd simply step over it to get in and out of the van ... no problem.... Until we got back to our upscale hotel, and proceeded to try to get out of the van.

Although I was trying to be very ladylike, I somehow got stuck! I'm a fairly small person, so I don't see how I could have gotten stuck, but I did! I couldn't go forward. I couldn't go backward. My boss' wife, seeing my plight, decided to help by grabbing one of my "up in the air" legs and pulling.

Even the bell captain came over and tried to assist. He grabbed my other leg ... but that didn't help. The Bell Captain was laughing so hard, he had tears streaming down his face, my sides were aching from laughter, and everyone in our group was laughing. But my body still wouldn't budge.

Just as a crowd of onlookers started to form, I finally managed to get loose. Which is a good thing. Renting a jaws of life can be expensive these days.

EMBARRASSING MOMENTS IN NURSERY RHYMES

"Look at it this way, Jill. If we hadn't tripped, what would Mother Goose have had to write about?"

Jack

"Mother, I asked you to call the exterminator weeks ago. Now the whole world's going to know about our spider problem!"

Little Miss Muffet

"Jack, if you don't quit sticking your thumb in the pies, they'll never let us eat at Denny's again."

Little Jack Horner's mom

"We don't mean to embarrass you, wolf, but your breath could knock over a house!"

The Three Little Pigs

"Look, lamb, I don't mind your following me to school, but that skirt and top you're wearing are just so 80s."

Mary

WHERE'D EVERYBODY GO?

Rev. Gene Paul

Once, while trying out for a pastoral position, I was in the middle of my sermon and trying my best to make a good impression when my glasses fell and hit the floor, knocking out one of the lenses. I didn't want to lose my momentum, so I simply bent over, picked them up, and put them back on. I continued preaching to the half of the congregation I could see, believing in faith that the other half was still there, too.

A HAIRY SITUATION

Jeanette Martinson

When I first accepted my new job as a psychotherapist for a large organization, I had to drive up to Chicago for about six days straight for training seminars. None of us knew each other when the sessions began, but by the end of the week we were a pretty close-knit group.

Late in the afternoon of the third day, my thoughts drifted to the two-hour drive home, my family, our dinner ... and the unruly strand of hair that was hanging down in my face! I had cut my bangs the night before, and had obviously missed a spot.

I thought about waiting for the next "break time" to run to the rest room, get out my nail clippers, and fix my hair. But the trainer was so absorbed in his talk on the side effects of Ativan that he didn't break soon enough. With every passing second, the hair seemed to grow a little longer.

The teacher droned on. I began counting the number of times I reached up and pushed it out of the way. When I reached fifty-six, I thought, "This is ridiculous. The bathroom is right across the hall. I will simply get a sheepish look that says, 'Sorry, I hate to leave this fascinating lecture, but I drank way too much Coke at lunch,' and leave the room quietly."

That was the plan.

I executed my departure perfectly. When I got to the rest room, I pulled out my nail clippers, located the offending strand (which wasn't too difficult since I'd been playing with it for half an hour), and reached up to clip it right off. But just as the clippers clamped shut, my fingers slipped and the nail clippers sprang back, hitting me by the corner of my eye.

My eyes watering, I put the weapon back in my purse and returned to the lecture, ready to move on to the various mood stabilizers on the market. As I entered the room, however, I felt every eye upon me. Now, I knew my pants were zipped, and toilet paper was not hanging anywhere. What was going on?

Suddenly one fellow trainee broke the silence. "What happened to *you?*" People started handing me napkins, and I soon discovered blood was running down my face from my recent injury. Whipping a mirror out of my purse, I saw that my nose was swollen and beginning to bruise.

Everyone awaited my answer. I always tell my kids to tell the truth, so I said sheepishly, "I cut my hair."

A gentleman wrapped some ice in a towel and responded, "With what? A butcher knife?"

We took a break at this point (Why couldn't I have just waited?), and everyone gathered in to hear the story of my bathroom massacre.

By the end of the week, we were all great friends. We had bonded.

And what did I learn from the embarrassing moment? To

67

be patient when I become obsessed with something, to not let vanity take control of my thoughts, and to go to a professional hair dresser once a month, even if it's just to cut my bangs!

"Nobody ever died of laughter."

Max Beerbohm

WELCOME TO OUR CHURCH

One Sunday a pastor wanted to urge his congregation to greet all the visitors to the service that day. So he asked the visitors to stand, then told the membership to "take a good look at these people and keep an eye on them after the service."

SPEECHLESS IN THE SANCTUARY

Cynthia Christenssen

While performing in a church play before a packed auditorium, my mind suddenly went totally blank. I knew my next line started with, "All I want to say...," but after that I had absolutely no recall whatsoever. So I turned to my costar and said, "All I want to say is ... all I want to say is ... I bet you know what I want to say!"

"In three words I can sum up everything I've learned about life: it goes on."

Robert Frost

Chapter 7

MISTAKEN IDENTITIES

The Lord will be your confidence and will keep your foot from being snared.

PROVERBS 3:26

"Even the fall of a dancer is a somersault."

Senegalese proverb

I never forget a name. Paul, Ann, Linda, Mary, Kevin, Mark, Bob—I know them all. Names are easy to remember. What's more difficult is remembering which names go with which faces.

In school my teachers were always forgetting my name. Most of them had already had my four older siblings in their classes, so they would often call me by one of their names.

My mother would even call me by their names. She'd just go down the list of names until she reached mine.

So if you find yourself forgetting names, too, don't feel bad. It happens to all of us, even the president of the United States ... now what was his name again?

WHO NEEDS NAME TAGS?

Once while attending a convention, my husband and I ran into a writer friend whom I had known for several years and my husband had met numerous times before at various functions. I could tell by the puzzled look on my husband's face, though, that he was having a difficult time placing this person. After talking, laughing, and reminiscing with him for about twenty minutes, my husband couldn't stand the mystery any longer. He finally just paused midsentence and asked, "Do I know you?"

HONEST, OFFICER...
Student

I was staying at my friend Abby's house. Her uncle was getting married that weekend and she invited me to come with her family to the wedding and reception. I was honored and I accepted the invitation gladly. The wedding went great, everything was beautiful, and we were all having a great time. At the reception, there was food, music, the whole works. Abby had an older sister, Hope, and two girl cousins who were about our age, so we all hung out together. It was getting pretty hot in the room, so we decided to step out and go to the rest room. When I was done, I saw a black purse on the floor behind one of the stalls and knew that Hope had a black purse, so I decided to play a trick on her. I slipped my foot under the door and pulled out the purse.

Suddenly a lady started screaming! I looked around and saw that Hope was right behind me. I had mistaken this innocent lady's purse for Hope's. I threw the purse back under the stall and ran out. I couldn't believe it. This lady probably thought she was being robbed!

For the rest of the reception I kept my feet under the table so whoever the poor woman was wouldn't recognize them!

I'D RECOGNIZE YOU ANYWHERE

Donna East, Comedian/Actress

Unfortunately, sometimes I have a very bad memory, which gets me into trouble. For example, if I meet someone and he tells me his name, I never remember it because I'm too busy thinking of the next thing to say. But I never thought it would happen with a face. A few years ago while waiting on tables in a very busy New York City restaurant, I walked up to this one particular table to take their order and tell them the specials of the day. Just as friendly as can be, the woman started talking to me as if she knew me. Her face was familiar, so I began to converse with her. On the inside, however, I was racking my brain to figure out who she was and how I knew her. Finally, embarrassed and with all honesty, I said, "I'm sorry. How do I know you?" As loud as can be, she said, "You don't recognize me? I'm your gynecologist!"

I was almost too embarrassed to even take her order. But I did. And yes, you guessed it. She ordered BBQ breast of chicken sandwich.

SORRY, NO PETS

When my grandaughter, Kiana, was about twenty months old, we took her and her mother, Nicole, with us on our cross-country trek from California to Tennessee. She fared rather well, considering all the car trouble we had. That is, except for this one particular restaurant experience.

It was at a cafeteria in Albuquerque. After we got our food and wheeled her high chair to our table, she decided to become ... well, a cat. That's right. A cat. She meowed through the entire meal and didn't break character even once. This, in spite of our repeated attempts to get her to stop. "Kiana, people are looking at us."

"Meow," is all she would say.

"Kiana, the waitress wants to know what you'd like to drink."

"Meow," was still her only answer. Which, I assume, meant she wanted a bowl of milk.

People were staring, the waitress was getting nowhere with her drink order, and we were baffled beyond belief. Didn't she know that in comedy you never milk a laugh this long?

But she didn't stop. "Meow, meeeeeow, meoooooooooow, meowwwwwwww, mmmmmmmmmmeow, meow, MEOW." It was like she was auditioning for a 9Lives commercial. She kept up the feline impersonation throughout the entire meal. It was embarrassing, but funny. She was definitely causing a scene, but there wasn't anything we could do about it. So, we simply ignored her antics and finished eating, hoping the people at the tables around us wouldn't report us for bringing a "pet" into the restaurant.

Once the meal was over and we walked outside, she became Kiana again, talking up a storm and not meowing once. In fact, she never even mentioned the "cat incident." ... Maybe it had something to do with that dog in the car next to us.

HUGS FOR FREE

C.P., Student

I like to hang on my mom because she's just the right size.

Once, at a theme park, while my family and I were waiting in line, I just sat down. After awhile I looked up and saw someone who looked liked my mom ... from the back. I started hanging on her, until this total stranger turned and looked at me and said, "You're nice but ..."

That's as far as I let her get!!! I ran to catch up with my family and was embarrassed for the rest of the day!

---

blush: verb 1. to become red in the face, as from shyness or shame

(from Webster's New World Dictionary)

BARKING UP THE WRONG STABLE

Rev. David Sloat

One Christmas I was given the role of a shepherd boy in my church's annual Christmas pageant. Not only was I to be in full biblical costume, but I was to carry Daisy, a white cockapoo dog, in my arms and pass her off as a lamb. Believe it or not, it worked. I made it all the way down the center aisle, up to the manger where "Baby Jesus" was lying, and then knelt without anyone suspecting that my beloved lamb was really a canine. Unfortunately, though, as soon as my knee hit the carpet, the dog let out a yelp, jumped out of my arms, and continued barking as she ran all the way back up the aisle, with me, in full shepherd's costume, chasing after her!

PASS THE POPCORN
Mark Christian, Youth Pastor

Years ago while I was at a movie theater, I left my date during the middle of the movie to go to the bathroom. When I came back to the dark theater I sat down in my seat, put my arm around my date, and asked "What'd I miss?" The deep voice of a long-haired male said with surprise, "Your seat."

OUT OF SYNC
Alicia Conover, Student

It was about 10:30 P.M. and my friends and I were at a hotel. We were doing our makeup at the time and we thought we saw the guys from 'N Sync. Their room was only about five rooms away from ours so, of course, we all took our lipstick and wrote "I love you!" all over our faces and on yellow pieces of paper and went running down the hall screaming and chasing after them. It wasn't them.... We ran a lot faster back to our room!

WHAT'S YOUR HURRY?
Anonymous Editor

Oddly enough, I had received manuscripts from two different people who were both named Matt Roberts. The first sent me his material in June. The second sent his in August. The first Matt called me during the second week of August, wanting an update. I thought he was the Matt Roberts whose manuscript had just arrived in my mail the week before, and I reacted to his impatience accordingly. Instead, it was the first Matt, who had done exactly what he should have done by waiting three months before inquiring about his manuscript. Unfortunately, however, I was a bit terse with him as I tried my best to explain that he needed to give editors TIME to even open the envelope, much less perform a complete evaluation of a project. I hung up and a few days went by, and the first Matt Roberts' manuscript surfaced on my desk. AAAAGGGGHHH! Needless to say, I called him back to apologize.

MONKEY BUSINESS
Phil Callaway, Author/Humorist

I happened to see a friend of mine at a mall and decided to sneak up behind him and make monkey faces until he turned around and saw me. Sensing someone behind him, he finally turned to see me in all my Planet of the Apes splendor. Only it wasn't my friend. I didn't know what to say to the total stranger with whom I was now nose to nose, so I just nodded and walked away. To this day, he's probably wondering if I ever got into therapy.

A BOB BY ANY OTHER NAME IS STILL A BOB
Bob Mills, Author and Veteran Staff Writer for Bob Hope

One night while preparing for our China special in 1979, I was with Bob Hope, going over some script changes in his bedroom at the Toluca Lake house. The phone rang, and as Bob was in the adjoining bathroom, he asked me to answer it. I lifted the receiver and said, "Yes?" A voice at the other end said, "Bob?" Instinctively, I said, "Yes."

Dolores, calling from her quarters at the other end of the house, began outlining her plans for an upcoming visit from Gerald Ford and his wife, Betty. She talked so fast that I couldn't stop her before she'd covered several topics regarding the visit. Finally, I broke in and said, "Dolores, this is Bob Mills. Your Bob is indisposed at the moment." There followed several seconds of silence. Long ones. Then, "Oh. Well, I'm glad he's in town. Tell him to give me a call when he gets a minute."

SNAKE DOUBLETAKE

One night when my husband was working late, I heard what sounded like a snake in our kitchen cupboard. I had been married only a few months and at only eighteen years old, I wasn't that used to being the woman of the house. The only thing I could think of to do was to call the police.

I stayed quite a distance away from the cupboard, just in case the snake decided to lunge out and try to strike me. When the policeman arrived, I explained the situation to him, then cautiously escorted him to the kitchen to where the slithery intruder was lying in wait.

"What makes you think it's a snake?" the policeman asked, making notations in his notebook, while approaching the cupboard ever so cautiously.

"It's a snake," I said confidently. "I heard it walking."

OK, so I lost all credibility from that moment on. And yes, it did turn out to be a mouse. Snake ... mouse ... when you get right down to it, there's really not that much difference, is there?

BOY, DID I GET A WRONG NUMBER

One of my most recent books is titled *Didn't My Skin Used to Fit?*
It's a humorous celebration of life, and shortly after I turned
in the manuscript to my editor, he wanted to call and tell me
how much he had enjoyed reading through it. Unfortunately,
though, he wasn't aware that I had moved and that someone
else now had my old California phone number.

"Is Martha there?" he asked the person who answered the
phone.

"Just a minute," the person said, then left to go get "Martha."
Evidently, another Martha now had the number. My editor figured this Martha was me, of course, so when the girl, obviously
a teenager, came on the line, he asked, "So, does your skin fit?"

"Excuse me?" the other Martha said.

Reality, as painful as it was, began to sink in. He had just asked
a total stranger, a teenage girl no less, if her skin fit. He apologized profusely, tried to explain why he'd asked such a question
in the first place, then finally just hung up and found my correct number.

MORE THAN HE BARGAINED FOR
"Arissa," Student

My mom and I were at a basketball game, watching my older
brother play, and my dad had gone out to the car to take care
of a business call. Mom thought that Dad had come back in
and sat down behind her, and as a good wife, she started mas-
saging his legs. Then out of the corner of her eye, she saw Dad
walk in. It clicked with her that the man's legs she was rubbing
were not the legs of her husband. She stopped with a jerk,
paused, and looked around. It was my school principal!

THE GETAWAY CAR

John Calhoun, Pastor
Olive Knolls Church of the Nazarene

In the spring of 1992 while serving as pastor of First Church of the Nazarene in Long Beach, California, I suffered the third loss of a car to thieves in my tenure at that assignment. This particular car was a Nissan 280ZX, with a personalized license tag to depict my pastoral position. It was inscribed "NAZ PAZ" and was therefore widely known and easily identified as mine.

The previously stolen cars had been found by police within a few days, one still intact and the other completely burned out. While I was awaiting some news concerning the whereabouts of the "NAZ PAZ" car, the infamous event known as the "Los Angeles Riots of '92" occurred. I assumed the police would be too occupied for a while to know anything of my car's status.

As I was watching the riots on television from the safety of my home, a well-intentioned lady in the church called, saying, "Why, Pastor, I'm glad to know you are home. I just saw your car on TV and was worried that you might get hurt," she said. I told her that I was safe at home and that my car had been stolen, and she seemed to accept the fact that I was not in the middle of the riots. I turned to the channel she was watching and saw my old "NAZ PAZ" license plate, plain as day, on the TV screen. The camera caught a perfect picture of someone looting an appliance store and jamming the 280ZX with every stolen television set it could hold.

The old "NAZ PAZ" went down in flames, as it was discovered a few days later completely burned out. But not before it had one shining moment as the getaway car for a looter in the riot of '92.

I wasn't able to get the word out to everyone who knew that car that I really was at home during the riots! But maybe this will help.

"The greatest mistake you can make in life is to be continually fearing you will make one."

E. Hubbard

Chapter 8

THE BEST-LAID PLANS

> *But you are a shield around me, O Lord; you bestow glory on me and lift up my head.*
>
> PSALM 3:3

"It is easy to forgive others their mistakes; it takes more grit to forgive them for having witnessed your own."

Jessamyn West

Have you ever planned a practical joke on someone only to have the actual execution of it backfire in your face? Or scheduled an outing and had everything that could possibly go wrong, go wrong? Maybe you stayed up all night studying for the wrong test at school, or showed up to class in your Winnie the Pooh costume because you thought your teacher had announced "Bear Day," only to find out that she had said "D.A.R.E. Day" instead.

No matter how hard we try, our best-laid plans don't always turn out the way we were hoping they would. But, if we allow them to, they can turn into something we'll laugh about ... eventually.

SPECIALITY DISHES

One night as a joke I decided to put all the scraps from my dinner preparation into a bowl and place it on the table along with the regular food to see if any of my dinner guests would notice. It looked awful. There were potato peelings, cucumber peelings, egg shells, scrapings from the mashed potato pan, meat juices from the skillet, and various other unappetizing food items.

We said grace, then began passing the bowls around the table while I waited patiently for everyone to erupt in laughter. But there was no eruption. Not one person even noticed. Apparently, the bowl of garbage didn't look all that different from other dishes I had served in the past.

Too embarrassed to admit my joke, I waited for the bowl to come around to me and took two scoops. Actually, it wasn't that bad.

I YAM WHAT I YAM

I should have known better, but it sounded reasonable at the time. Someone suggested to me that a good way to get rid of unsightly cellulite was by using one of those vibrating belts. They even suggested that in addition to using it on the usual body parts, I should try it on my upper arms, since that's where most of my cellulite seemed to be gathering.

So, I decided to give it a try. I climbed up onto the platform, strapped the belt around my arms, and leaned into it. It seemed to work fine, shaking my arms as much as they could possibly be shaken. I couldn't see any immediate change, but was sure that I would eventually.

Eventually didn't take very long to arrive. When I woke up the next morning, I looked in the mirror and couldn't believe my eyes. The cellulite was gone! It was... how shall I put this... now in a heap down by my elbows! No, that's not a misprint. Apparently, all that shaking had caused my upper arm fat to slide south. Instead of being up north where it belonged, it was now resting comfortably at my elbows. I looked like Popeye.

When I showed my newly acquired abnormality to my doctor, he studied it for several minutes before commenting, "How'd you say you did this again?"

I repeated what I had done and why, and he made some notes in my chart, then called in one of his partners to examine me as well. "How'd you say you did this again?" his partner asked.

I was both embarrassed at my stupidity and depressed at what I had done to my body. I no longer wanted to wear short sleeves, for fear of being accosted by Popeye groupies and hounded for autographs. And forget swimsuits. I looked like a shark had already gotten to me.

My arms stayed like that for two years! Then, one morning, to my amazement, I looked in the mirror and noticed that my upper arm fat had just as mysteriously returned to its rightful position. Without warning, without fanfare, it went home, like the swallows returning to Capistrano. I was back to my normal self, cellulite and all. I still don't know why my unruly fat decided to venture off to regions unknown in the first place. It was some sort of medical oddity. But I'm glad that the whole incident is behind me. I never did, though, get rid of that craving for spinach.

TOUGH SECRETARY

Gene Perret
Emmy-Winning Comedy Writer and Book Author

One evening, my wife, Joanne, and I were going to dinner at a nearby restaurant. We decided to leave the children alone for the first time. They were about the right age, and we were close and could get home in a relatively short time, if needed. However, I did instruct them not to tell anyone that their parents were out. I said, "If anyone calls, tell them Daddy's in the shower."

Sure enough, Bob Hope called. My daughter Terry answered the phone, and when Bob asked for me, she dutifully told him I was in the shower. Bob wasn't letting me off the hook that easily. He said, "Well, tell him it's Bob Hope calling. He'll come to the phone."

She hung up on him.

REVERSE BOWLING

One night recently, my daughter-in-law Crystal, my son Tony, my husband Russ, and I all went bowling together. For some reason, the pin machine wasn't working properly and was dropping all the pins onto the floor, instead of setting them up neatly for the next bowler. We were getting spares and strikes without even having to work for them.

A few times, however, we had to roll the ball down the alley to get the pins to reset themselves. Or at least that was the plan. Once when Crystal did this, the metal bar came down at the precise moment her ball reached the pin area. Her ball then hit the metal bar, reversed itself, and came flying back up the alley. There was so much power in that ball that it shot all the way back to the benches where we were sitting! My son managed to stop the runaway "cannon ball" in midflight after it came barreling into his leg, thus saving the rest of us from becoming the first reverse strike on record!

RIDE AT YOUR OWN RISK

Ginger Shew, Theatrical Makeup Artist

For years, I never told anyone how I broke my tailbone. I confess it now—I fell out of a grocery cart. I was twenty-three. My roommate and I were bored and broke, and it was after midnight on a hot night in a small town. The cart had been out in the parking lot for days, enticing us.

We were going to take turns going for rides—at least that was the plan. We whizzed around the lot awhile, then went to do a turnaround in the street, but a small pebble did us in. I went down, heard a snap, and knew I was in trouble. The pain was enough to make me think I'd been paralyzed.

As I lay there in the street with my feet still in the cart, its little wheels spinning, my friend said in an urgent whisper, "GET UP! People are coming!"

People *were* coming, but I didn't care. "I can't ..." I moaned. Even a police officer drove by, but kept on going. He either was used to seeing this sort of thing, or just didn't know how to word it in a report.

Eventually, I was able to hobble to my feet and limp back to the apartment, where we worked out our story: "I fell...." We always let the listener finish the sentence.

A hospital security guard confessed this story. One night when a big football game was on television, he and a coworker found a deserted room in the hospital, locked the door, turned out the lights, and sat down to watch the game. This was a room that was frequently used for various group meetings, but apparently no one was using it that night, so as long as they had their walkie-talkies, they figured they were home free.

Midway through the game, however, they heard someone trying to get in the door. From the voices, they could tell it was a group of people, and deduced that a meeting was indeed scheduled there that evening.

They were trapped. There was no way out other than through that door. They were going to have to come up with some sort of excuse, they figured, for being in that room with the door locked and the television on. While they were desperately trying to think of one, they heard one of the people say, "Let's go find a security guard." Since these two security guards were the only ones on duty that night, they knew the only way out of their predicament was to open the door and face the music. And find out the football score later.

WHO? ME? LOST?
Christan Nicole McCoy

One unforgettable evening during my freshman year in college, When I was just getting a taste of true freedom, I decided to take some of my friends and exercise my right to stay out past curfew. The plan was to boldly take the metro to Chicago and upon arrival do "whatever."

Thoughts of hitting the malls, walking around downtown, and maybe going to a comedy club or two danced in my head. I certainly didn't know my way around Chicago, and neither did any of my friends, but even though my Resident Assistant suggested we plan something out or simply wait to take a bigger group, I assured her we'd be fine. After all, I could handle anything!

With my dressy clothes, overly confident attitude, and reluctant friends, we hopped in my car and started driving ... only to soon realize that we didn't know our way to the metro. We stopped at a gas station and asked directions to the train station. Train station, metro—what's the difference, right?

We drove confidently to the train station and hopped aboard. After paying a ludicrous price for getting up to Chicago, my friends began to get worried and started asking questions. Being assured that I could NOT make a mistake, I told them everything was fine. It wasn't long before we began getting funny looks from people who overheard we were taking the train to Chicago for the night. We even got a chuckle out of a conductor, who told us there was no way we were going to get back to Kankakee the same night. OK, I began to doubt myself ... but only a little.

The train arrived in Chicago and soon we were walking around Union Station. My friends and I started looking at schedules as to when we could catch the train back to Kankakee, only to discover that the conductor was correct. There wasn't a train going back to Kankakee that night.

Still, I was confident. I'd find us another way back, but wouldn't worry about it until the time came. For now, I just wanted to have fun!

After walking around for about an hour, finding nothing in the immediate area to do, not sure where we were, and listening to my friends' doubts about getting any sleep that night, I'd finally had it. "Fine! I'll find us a way back!" I said.

Our only hope of getting home that night was to catch a bus. Not only was that going to be unpleasant, it also meant more expense for us. (In college terms, about twelve laundry loads!) While trying to find the bus station, though, we got lost. Determined not to let my friends see me scared or admit any defeat, I stopped a man on the street and asked directions. He gave them to us, but not until I paid him twenty bucks. (I could have bought a Thomas Guide for twenty bucks!)

When we finally arrived at the bus station, we discovered that the next bus for Kankakee didn't leave until 8:00 the following morning! Our evening of fun, excitement, and freedom had turned into a nightmare. And who was the writer/director/producer of this nightmare? Me! You would think at this point that I would have given in. But no, I insisted we spend the night at the bus station and tell our Resident Assistant that we were having too much fun to leave Chicago. After all, bus stations can be fun, right?

Finally, my friend Kelley stepped in and (against my will!) called our RA, Valerie, and confessed our plight. I was mortified. The very person who had told us not to go, the one I had looked in the face and told, "We're going and we'll be fine," was coming to get us out of this bind.

I've learned some good lessons from this. I will no longer ignore advice given to me out of care and concern. I will confess a lot sooner when I don't know something. And I've learned that if you want to ride the metro, you don't ask directions to the train. Life just works out better that way.

STRANDED

On my third try for my driver's license, I had the misfortune of taking one of the family cars that wasn't exactly working correctly. The problem was that it tended to stall out every time you turned the steering wheel too far to the left or right. Even with that handicap, the driving test seemed to be going well— that is, until we got to the three-point turn. I stopped counting the number of times I had to restart the engine when I got to nine. I don't know if it was that, or my driving skills, but not only did he fail me for yet another time, but he even got out and walked all the way back to the DMV!

CHECKS AND BALANCES
Frank Bush
Los Angeles City Building Inspector

A number of years ago, I was the treasurer for my church. One of my responsibilities was to count and make the bank deposit of the weekly offerings. One week I knew I wasn't going to be able to make the deposit on Monday, so I decided to do it on Sunday night instead.

I started working on the deposit at the church, but it was getting late in the evening and since I didn't want to be there alone, I decided to take the offering home to complete it.

When I got home, I counted all the cash and checks and made out the deposit slips. I then put the cash and checks into the bank deposit bag, got into my car, and proceeded to drive to the bank to put the deposit in their twenty-four-hour drop. Suddenly, though, I realized I had forgotten to stamp the back of the checks with the church's bank stamp with the account number on it. So I went back into the house, sat down at my desk, and put the bank stamp on the back of them. I then headed to the bank and put the deposit bag into their twenty-four-hour drop.

When I got home, I sat down at my office desk, picked up the church's deposit stamp, and suddenly realized I had accidentally used the bank deposit stamp for my construction company instead! (Fortunately for me the church bank was different than mine, so it wouldn't have gotten deposited into my account. But still ...)

I felt sick. I couldn't sleep all night. I was at the bank when it opened on Monday morning. The bank manager assured me that the checks would be credited to the church account even with my construction company stamp on it. I was terrified, though, of what people might think when they got their bank statements and saw my construction company stamp on the back of their checks. I had to call each one of them and explain what had happened. I even had the bank manager's name and telephone number on hand in case they wanted to call and verify what I had told them.

Wow! What a few agonizing days that was! All went well until the following Sunday, when I was counting the offering with the ushers and one of them said, "Hey, look. There's a check for one dollar in the offering made out to Frank Bush Construction Company!" I laughed hysterically. The person who wrote the check (Martha Bolton) was a recipient of one of my explanation phone calls. She later told me that she figured that's where all of the offerings were going anyway, so she was just going to save time and make the check out directly to me.

"Regret for things we did can be tempered by time; it is regret for the things we did not do that is inconsolable."

Sydney J. Harris

Chapter 9

BLESSED ARE THE MERCIFUL

> Blessed are the merciful, for they will be shown mercy.
>
> MATTHEW 5:7

"What lies behind us and what lies ahead of us are tiny matters compared to what lives within us."

Oliver Wendell Holmes

The only thing worse than having an embarrassing moment is having it in front of an audience.

Witnesses. It doesn't matter whether it's an audience of one or one thousand. The fact that any other living person saw us at our most bumbling of moments can be mortifying.

Will they laugh at us or with us? Will our fumbled words or thoughtless act be written up in one of those Internet chain letters that circle the globe? Will we be in one of the featured tapes on *America's Funniest Home Videos?* Will we go down in history for our embarrassing moment, no matter how many Pulitzer or Nobel Prizes we're awarded?

Or will our audience simply feel for us, understand our humanity, and laugh with us?

Most of us don't care when others laugh with us. In fact, having others join us in a good laugh is one of the true joys of life. The key word here, though, is "with."

Being laughed "at" is a different story altogether. No one enjoys being ridiculed or mocked, or having their foible be the subject matter for the table conversation two rows over. Being laughed at is what makes embarrassing moments turn into devastating ones. If we let them.

When Ronald Reagan was running for president of the United States, there was some concern over his age. He knew his opponent was going to use this issue against him in an upcoming debate, so he beat him to the punch by saying, and I'm paraphrasing, "Age will not be a factor in this campaign. I will not use my opponent's youth and inexperience against him."

By poking fun at himself first, the presidential candidate took the negative impact out of any political sound bite that could have come out that night. And he ended up winning the election.

Abraham Lincoln was also skilled at turning the humor on himself and diffusing an accusation or criticism. He was once quoted as rebutting someone's comment with, "If I were two-faced, would I be wearing this one?"

We can follow these examples and do the same thing with our embarrassing moments. If we laugh at our own mistakes or shortcomings first, we beat others to the punch. Now they have the option to join in and laugh with us. Or they can laugh at us. But if they choose the latter, it won't matter, because our own laughter has already stated that we know we're not perfect. Their pointing out that fact to us or to others is simply a waste of time.

Just as we prefer that others laugh with us about our foibles, we need to be that kind of friend to others, too. We need to ask ourselves how we react when we witness someone else's most embarrassing moment. When they knock over that pitcher of root beer, are we the kind of friend who goes and gets some paper towels to help them clean it up, or do we just stand off to the side and giggle?

When all their schoolbooks come tumbling out of their locker, do we walk over and help them pick them up, or do we just thank God it didn't happen to us and walk on to our next class?

The next time you witness someone else's embarrassing moment, put yourself in their place. Laughter is always better when everyone gets to enjoy it.

WHERE AM I?

Mark Lowry, Entertainer/Songwriter

While performing in Milwaukee one night, I came to a place in my act where I sing the song "Bein' Happy." At the end of the song, I always scream out the name of the city where I happen to be, and ask the audience if they're happy. For instance, if I'm in New York, I scream, "NEW YORK CITY, IS EVERYBODY HAPPY?" And the audience will usually scream "YEAAAH!" If I'm in Los Angeles, I scream, "LOS ANGELES, IS EVERY-BODY HAPPY?" and they'll answer, "YEAAAH!" and so on.

On this particular night in Milwaukee, though, when I got to the part where I was supposed to scream, "MILWAUKEE, WISCONSIN, IS EVERYBODY HAPPY?" my mind went on vacation. I had no idea where in the world I was. I knew it started with an "M," but that's all I knew.

So, I quickly ran all the cities I knew that started with the letter M through my brain and chose one. I screamed, "MINNEAPOLIS, MINNESOTA, IS EVERYBODY HAPPY?"

Not one person answered. They didn't say "Yeah!" They didn't say "No." They just stared at me. Maybe they were waiting for the Minneapolis throng to start applauding. But no one was from Minneapolis, so no one applauded.

All five thousand people just sat there with their mouths gaping open. It was too late to do anything about it except keep on singing, and wonder if that night in Minneapolis, Minnesota, *was everybody happy?*

OOH LA LA

It's not just my voice that has kept me from having a music career (when I sing in the shower, Mr. Clean gets up and leaves the room). I have a slight problem with stage presence, too.

When my sister and I were asked to sing a duet at church, I had my own public giggle fest. She was to take the solo and I was to sing "ooooohhhhh" as backup. I felt so silly singing "ooooohhhhh" that I got tickled and giggled through the rest of the song. I mean GIGGLED! Every time I pursed my lips and tried to get out "ooooohhhhh," I lost it.

It was the kind of giggle where you try your best to hold in the laughter while your face turns beet red, your cheeks swell up, and finally you just explode. I giggled through an entire two verses and three choruses!

Maybe that's when I decided that comedy was my calling, not music.

APPLAUSE, APPLAUSE

The night my mother attended a Bob Hope taping, I arranged for her to have special VIP seating. It was only a few rows from the front, and in direct view of Bob. I could tell my mother was enjoying Bob's opening monologue because after every joke she would not only laugh, but clap as well. We're talking after every single joke! She would laugh, then try her best to lead the audience in applause. At first it wasn't that noticeable, but it went on for the entire forty-five-minute monologue. Bob hadn't met her yet, so he didn't know who she was. All he knew was that there was a woman clapping after every one of his jokes. He wasn't complaining, mind you. But no comedian gets that much applause. It got to where he would say the joke, then wait for her clapping to start.

After the show, I started to ask my mother about the clapping, but didn't have to because she quickly volunteered, "I didn't know which jokes were yours, so I clapped at them all!"

Mothers are wonderful, aren't they?

THE SHOW MUST GO ON
Stacy Beam, Singer/Songwriter/Pianist

It was my second year of college, and the head of the music department asked me to perform in front of the student body with the prestigious college show band that had, incidentally, recently been featured on *The Tonight Show.* I was thrilled to find out that I would be closing the show as Elvis, dressed in full satin sequined jumpsuit. The night arrived and the show was going beautifully. The dean of the college, along with thousands of students, was enjoying every minute of it. By the time my turn came to perform and I could hear the band begin that familiar theme from 2001, I was about to explode with excitement. This was the kind of night every performer lives for.

From "Blue Suede Shoes" to "Love Me Tender," the audience was in my hands. I was Elvis. For that night, anyway. Then came the final push of "American Trilogy," and I dramatically went down on one knee to bring it on home. As I was about to rise and deliver the final big note, however, my white patent leather boot slipped on what might have been a leak from the trombone's spit valve and I heard a great pop, indicating that I had just torn a major piece of cartilage in my knee, rendering me immobile and in tremendous pain. As I looked up at the band director, I was not greeted with a sympathetic look, nor did I hear a call for someone to come and drag "Elvis" off the stage. All I saw was the microphone shoved so close to my face that it nearly touched my nose, and all I heard was a voice saying, "You started this, you've gotta finish it!" So from the ground I belted, "His truth is marching oooooon."

Someone told me the dean thought it was all part of the show, but I think he was just being nice. The crowd did applaud as I was carried off the stage with my gold lamé-lined cape flying in the wind, and I think a few people sent flowers to my room after the orthoscopic surgery that repaired my knee. Not much could be done to repair my badly injured ego, though.

SOMETHING OLD, SOMETHING NEW ... SOMEONE BLUE
Heidi Saxton, Author and Editor

I've been serving various churches since I was twelve—as organist, pianist, choir director, you name it. So, naturally, when my sister asked me to sing for her wedding, it never occurred to me that I wouldn't be able to do it.

I should probably mention it was my younger sister.

I should also probably mention that I had just broken up with my own boyfriend.

Can you see where this is going?

So there we all were. The flowers were beautiful. The bridal party was radiant. My parents beamed proudly from the front row. And at the appointed moment, I stood up to sing.

But nothing came out. I cleared my throat and cued the organist to start over. Still nothing. I looked at the bride, the groom, then the ringless fourth finger of my left hand. At that moment my eye twitched and all the fluid that should have been in my throat started gushing from my tear ducts. We're talking monsoon magnitude. I tried my best to appear happy for my sister, and I really was, but it was hard to convince anyone in the front rows of that while they were reaching for floatation devices and opening their umbrellas!

Somebody finally handed me a tissue, and somehow I composed myself enough to get through that song before beating a hasty retreat to the church cloakroom to finish my cry in private.

I remember being grateful that no one teased me. And now, years later, I can look back and laugh at that situation. Not just because I'm happily married to a wonderful man, but because whenever I feel unsure of myself, I just insert that video into my VCR and watch it over and over again. After all, if I made it through that day, I can make it through anything!

AN ACTOR'S NIGHTMARE
Robert J. Hanley, Actor

I was doing a play in San Diego, a matinee, live performance, to a packed house. One of the stars of the show and I had a scene together every night, just the two of us, center stage with 450 people watching. At one point, with me sitting on a couch, the scene is supposed to go like this:

ACTRESS
(with regret, she says to him)
I've treated you dishonestly and now I feel guilty.

ME
(bewildered, I say to her)
How? I've been away.

But in this particular performance, the scene went like this:

ACTRESS

(with regret, she says to him)

I've treated you dishonestly and now I feel guilty.

ME

(I forget my line. I'm in a panic. I don't know what to say or what state I'm in. In less-than immediately, I'm asking God for help. He sends it by way of an ad lib. I "calmly" repeat her line back to her ...)

You've treated me dishonestly and now you feel guilty...?

(I silently thank God for helping me.)

ACTRESS

(Eyes bulging, looking down at me in shock, wondering what's going on. She's thinking, "That's not the line! I'll kill you." She softly says ...)

Yes.

ME

(I STILL DON'T KNOW MY LINE. AHHH. WHERE AM I???? But then, God comes through again, as I simply say to her ...)

And...?

We both remembered all of our lines after that and finished the scene.

And I'm alive to tell about it.

A LITTLE MORE TO YOUR RIGHT
Ashley Fauls

Recently, I was in an Easter performance at my church. I know sign language and was signing the performance in case anyone in the audience was hearing impaired.

My teacher wanted an older man in my church to tape me, to later show her class at school. Apparently, I was standing too far to the left and was not in the camera's view. The man started waving his hand and asking my teacher to get me to move over.

I didn't know what way she meant when she whispered "Move over," so I moved farther left. After several minutes of my scooting in all directions, she finally grabbed the hem of my dress and simply dragged me across the stage to where I needed to be.

A LOSS FOR WORDS
Phil Callaway, Author

When I was being interviewed on Canada's most watched morning television show, the host asked, "Phil, what are a few keys to being a really good father?"

I said, "Well, it's like Martin Luther once said ... Um ... he said that ... um ... that we should never forget what he said ... oh boy ... I can't remember. What's your next question?"

"You don't drown by falling in the water; you drown by staying there."

Edwin Louis Cole

OUCH

"A composer whose music is better than it sounds."

Mark Twain,
speaking about composer Richard Wagner

"A fellow with the inventiveness of Albert Einstein, but with the attention span of Daffy Duck."

Tom Shales,
speaking about actor Robin Williams

"Can't act. Slightly bald. Can dance a little."

Anonymous remarks written on
Fred Astaire's first screen test

"Calvin Coolidge didn't say much, and when he did, he didn't say much."

Will Rogers,
on President Calvin Coolidge

"Handel is only fourth-rate. He is not even interesting."

Peter Tchaikovsky,
speaking about George Frederick Handel

"We don't like their sound, and guitar music is on the way out."

Decca Recording Company,
on why they rejected the Beatles

Chapter 10

TELL ME YOU DIDN'T

Those who look to him are radiant; their faces are never covered with shame.

PSALM 34:5

"I am being frank about myself in this book. I tell of my first mistake on page 850."

Henry Kissinger

Ever wish you could press a button and rewind a certain moment of your life? Or a day? Or maybe even a whole year? Wouldn't it be great to be given another chance to say the correct thing, another opportunity to make those right decisions? This time we wouldn't stand so close to the edge of the walrus exhibit that we fall in and become a part of his act; this time we'd read the assigned chapter in our history books before our teacher asks, "Who won the Spanish-American War?" and we answer, "The Taco Bell Chihuahua." This time we'd get it right.

Unfortunately, though, life works only in the Play position. There isn't any Rewind button. Or Fast Forward. We can't erase those embarrassing moments from our lives. We can only learn to laugh about them.

THE DRINKS ARE ON HIM

Diantha Ain, Writer/Actress

When I came to California in 1949, I was an aspiring young actress fresh out of The Dramatic Workshop in New York City. I had an agent, but I needed a real job in order to survive until an acting job came up, so I became a carhop.

At that time, Simon's Drive-In Restaurants were the biggest and busiest in the area. Although I was hired in Hollywood, I was sent to work at the one in Beverly Hills at the corner of Linden Drive and Wilshire Boulevard.

Balancing the trays and hooking them into their places was tricky, but I soon mastered the skill. The inside trays went into the car on the passenger's side or in the rear windows and sat just over the lap. They hooked into the crack by the window and adjusted with a knob against the inside of the door. The outside trays attached outside. The window needed to be up a few inches so the tray could clip over it, then a metal brace under the tray was slid until its rubber base rested against the car. It took some experience to do it smoothly and quickly.

Occasionally, movie stars stopped by for refreshments, and one afternoon Gene Kelly drove up in my station. I tried to be nonchalant about taking his order for a chocolate shake. I forget what the woman with him ordered. I prepared an outside tray with water and napkins, and when the order came up, I loaded it on the tray. As I walked to the car, I stared at the vanilla shake in the tall, cone-shaped glass and sensed a mistake had been made, but by then I was at the car.

In my nervous state, as I clipped the tray to his window and slid the brace against the door, the vanilla shake went sailing right through the window into Gene Kelly's lap! I could have died, I was so embarrassed, but he couldn't have been nicer.

After apologizing profusely, I brought him napkins and a cloth to clean it up. I couldn't do much else to help, considering where it had landed. Then I brought him the chocolate shake he had ordered.

I had always admired Gene Kelly for his magnificent dancing, but, from then on, I admired him even more for being a really nice, and very forgiving, man.

PATIENCE, PLEASE

When I was in high school, I was on an after-school bowling league. I enjoyed bowling and even entertained the notion of becoming a professional bowler. For a week or so at least. That is, until the one game when I got impatient waiting for my ball to come back through the ball return shoot. For some reason I got it into my head that if I put my hand inside the circular hole, I could grab hold of the ball when it got close and help it on out.

Unfortunately, though, there wasn't enough room in that hole for both my hand *and* the ball. When the ball did come, it started pressing against my hand at full force. The power of the conveyor belt was so strong that I couldn't push the ball back to get my hand out.

The whole incident was surreal. I remember asking my teammates to tell the manager to shut down the system so the pain would stop. They did, and he did, and I was finally able to get my poor bruised hand back.

Needless to say, I gave up my dreams of becoming a professional bowler. Unless, of course, the Red Cross wants to sponsor me.

CLASS IN SESSION

A hospital near my home rents out some of its rooms to groups for their monthly meetings. One night, a lady approached one of the security officers and asked, "Where does the 'Freedom From Fat' class meet?"

The security officer, figuring it was some sort of joke, replied, "Down at the Dairy Queen."

She wasn't joking. When the embarrassed officer realized this, he got the information for her, then decided it might be a good idea to stop by the Dairy Queen on his way home and pick up a job application ... just in case he'd soon be needing it.

NOT MY BEST JOB INTERVIEW
Phil Callaway, Author

I phoned a guy once who was hiring people to paint for him. When I called, a high-pitched voice answered the other end of the line. "Hello. Is your husband there?" I asked. There was a brief pause on the other end of the line. "I am the husband." Somehow, I still got the job.

A SOLEMN MOMENT
K. Kurz, Student

After a friend's funeral, there was a dinner to which only close friends and family were invited. My family and I went, and after I had eaten, I went to get the good stuff—dessert. There was only cake with lots of icing on it. After I had picked up my piece of cake, I went to talk to my friends who were huddled in a little group. I can't remember exactly what we were talking about but I do remember that I was in the way of a guy who was trying to walk past me. When I stepped aside so he could go by, I ended up stepping on my sister's foot ... lost my balance ... the cake went flying ... and I ended up on the floor! The cake, with all the icing, was on the carpet and just about ended up in one girl's face. Not my most graceful moment.

JUST ORDER, PLEASE
Student

My mom, brother, and I went out for lunch. There was a waiter who I thought was really cute, and I told my mom. He had the most gorgeous smile and blue eyes. He wasn't our waiter, but when he was passing by our table, my mom said, "Excuse me," and he turned around and answered, "Yes, Ma'am?"

Then my mom proceeded to tell him, "My daughter thinks you're cute." I thought I would die, and I turned as red as a tomato. He just looked at me and smiled. Then, the rest of the time we were at the restaurant, he would smile at me whenever he passed.

I never tell my mother when I think a guy is cute, anymore.

MAKING A SPLASH!
Judy Bush, Homemaker/Mother of Four

While chaperoning for our church youth group at Raging Waters in Southern California, I went down a steep and winding slide, hit the pool of water at the bottom, and rolled a few times. When I finally oriented myself, I was sitting in about a foot of water with the top of my one-piece bathing suit down around my waist.

The moral? When you're going down a water slide, make sure you travel at the same speed as your bathing suit.

"The rate at which a person can mature is directly proportional to the embarrassment he can tolerate."

Doug Engelbart

BANK ENCOUNTERS OF THE EMBARRASSING KIND
Kathi Mills-Macias, Author

For about two years I had been going to a gym and, although it was coed, my aerobics class was all women. Which was a good thing considering those silly workout outfits you have to wear.

Clyde (not his real name, for soon-to-be-obvious reasons), several years younger than I, was the only male employee at the gym. He was such a permanent fixture, I hardly noticed him anymore, once I'd been going there for a while.

Throughout the time I attended the gym, I don't remember ever having seen Clyde anyplace else in town, so I was surprised to see him walk into the bank one Friday afternoon. Waiting (along with what seemed to be about a million other people) to cash a check for the weekend, I was next in line for the first available teller when Clyde walked in. He spotted me, did a double take, then started walking my way.

"Kathi," he said, grinning from ear to ear. "I wasn't sure it was you at first. I didn't recognize you with your clothes on."

Ever seen the commercial where, when E.F. Hutton speaks, everyone else stops and listens? If so, you know just what happened in the bank that day. You could have heard a pin drop. As I stood there, turning eight shades of crimson and wondering whether I would make the situation worse by trying to explain to everyone that he was referring to the fact that the only other place he had ever seen me was at the gym in my workout outfit, I decided the best thing to do was to forget about cashing my check, run out the door, jump into my car, go straight home, pack a suitcase, and leave town—forever.

Well, I did everything but pack a suitcase and leave town, but I will admit this—I changed banks, and I didn't renew my membership at the gym that year. I told myself it was because the interest rates were better at the new bank and it was cheaper to use one of my aerobic tapes at home, but ... well, I think you understand.

RECOVERING FROM RECOVERY
Mary Scott, Poet/Writer

When my son was three, I had a hysterectomy and was in the hospital for five days. Upon my return, George "punished" me for abandoning him (it didn't help that his father toilet trained him during my absence). George dumped a semi-set bowl of green Jell-O on the kitchen floor and cut up one of his father's shirts. He emptied his father's hairspray bottle and refilled it with water (which made Dad's hair frizz). One afternoon, he even brought the hose in and flooded the large kitchen.

To top it all, when I ventured out one morning to retrieve the newspaper, George locked the door behind me. He dragged a chair to the window and gleefully watched me struggle with the ladder, which I propped below his bedroom window, near the neighbors' driveway. As I was inching my way up the ladder, the neighbors walked out of their house and got into their car. They waved to me as they drove off, seemingly unfazed by the sight of me clad in my purple bathrobe and clutching my stitches.

George and I survived my recovery, but I never went out in my bathrobe again, and it took a long time before I could face those neighbors.

FYI
Did you know there's a city in Minnesota named "Embarrass"?

GOOD GRADES AREN'T EVERYTHING

When my son was in elementary school, he brought home a report that he had written at school. The story was on ants, and he had received an A. I was thrilled at the grade, but still say he could have rewritten the closing sentence, the one that said, "Some ants live in the dirt, some ants live in the grass, and the rest of the ants live at our house."

"Men show their character in nothing more clearly than by what they find laughable."

Anonymous

110

Chapter 11

SURPRISE, SURPRISE, SURPRISE

> *The troubles of my heart have multiplied; free me from my anguish.*
>
> PSALM 25:17

"Anyone who has never made a mistake has never tried anything new."

Albert Einstein

The secret to good comedy is the element of surprise. A comedian should never "telegraph" the joke. In other words, he or she wants to lead the audience in a certain direction, then take a sudden turn and surprise them with the punch line. The audience should never see the joke coming. It's these kinds of surprise twists that garner the biggest belly laughs from an audience.

Some of our funniest and most embarrassing moments are ones we don't see coming, either. They take us totally by surprise. We count on one thing happening, but something else completely unexpected happens instead. We take that unexpected turn. We get surprised.

Or maybe someone else surprises us, such as is the case with practical jokes. I've played a lot of practical jokes on people throughout my life. This chapter includes my confession of a few of them.

But whether it's a practical joke or some other kind of surprise that causes our embarrassing moment, the simple fact is this—surprises keep us on our toes.

A LITTLE NUDGE

When I was working as secretary of my church, one of my duties was to do the weekly newsletter. I enjoyed this part of the job, as it was a good outlet for my creativity. That creativity, however, did tend to get me into trouble every once in a while.

Like the time Juanita Hodges, a wonderful Christian woman and longtime Sunday school teacher, asked me to put something in the newsletter for her. She was substitute teaching for the pastor's Sunday school class while he was away on vacation.

That first week, though, the turnout wasn't what she thought it should be. So she stopped by the church office and asked if I'd mind putting a "little nudge" in the newsletter, encouraging the students to remain faithful to the pastor's class during his absence.

I assured her I would.

By the time Monday morning arrived, my mischievousness was at an all-time high. I typed the regular newsletter containing a polite nudge, but then I typed up a custom newsletter for Juanita that only she would receive. I included a graphic drawing of a woman jumping up and down in a huff, and next to it I wrote in bold type, "Juanita Hodges Says: Get Out of That Bed!" I went on then with my custom text, saying things like "Just because the pastor's away, that doesn't mean you can sleep in on Sunday morning! What do you think I'm here for?

112

My health?" I continued for a few more paragraphs, then, giggling to myself, addressed it to Juanita and dropped it in the mail.

By midweek, I'd forgotten all about it. That is, until I received a telephone call from Tommy Thompson, one of the deacons of the church.

"Martha," he said, "I just got a strange phone call from Juanita Hodges."

"Really?" I asked, having completely forgotten about the newsletter.

"She's pretty distraught. She keeps saying she can't face her class on Sunday because of what was in the newsletter. But I've read and reread the newsletter and I don't know what she's talking about. I didn't see anything in there that was out of line. Do you think she needs a vacation?"

Finally, it dawned on me. The newsletter! I gasped, then started laughing and confessed what I had done. I also promised to immediately call Juanita and explain the situation to her. I did so, and we all had a good laugh over the incident. Of course, they're all pretty happy I'm putting my creativity into books now, instead of church newsletters!

DENTAL CARE

When my family and I posed for pictures for the church directory, we had the photographer take a family portrait as well. We liked how it turned out, and had them enlarge the proof to a nice 20" x 24" size to hang on the wall above our fireplace.

A few weeks later, when the portrait arrived in the mail, I excitedly opened it and prepared to put it into the wood frame that I had already purchased for it. I happened to notice, though, that there was something different about the picture. For some reason, it didn't look quite like the proof the photographer had shown us. Something was missing. What was it? What was it?

Ah, yes! Of course. My husband's TEETH! For some reason, my husband had no teeth. He has teeth, all his teeth, but in the picture he didn't have a single one! He was flashing a big toothless grin.

The next morning I took it back to the studio to complain. They shouldn't have given me a hard time. But then, the story wouldn't be in this book, would it?

"Are you sure your husband has teeth?" they asked.

"Yes, I'm sure."

"All of them?"

"He has teeth," I insisted.

"Maybe he forgot to put them in for the picture."

"He doesn't take them out!" I couldn't believe they weren't taking my word for it. I reached into my purse and took out other pictures of my husband. "See, there they are. I'm not kidding you. He has teeth."

She was still a little suspicious, but agreed to send the portrait back and have "teeth added." I kind of wish I still had that picture, though. It might be fun to color the teeth in myself and change the color scheme with the seasons.

A LOVE BALLAD
Lance Montalto, Comedian

While working at a comedy theater in Pigeon Forge, Tennessee, I had a solo part in the gospel number "Just Inside the Gate." I had a slight problem remembering all the words to the second verse so I printed them out and taped them to the stage. As a joke one night, Johann (our stage man) pulled up the words to the song and changed them without my knowledge. As I stepped forward to sing my verse, I looked down and noticed that he had rewritten all the words leaving me babbling due to the fact that the new lyrics had several "ooh baby, baby's" in them. Somehow I managed to make it through the song without breaking into a fit of laughter.

ALL FIRED UP
Al Fike, Comedian

Back in my little hometown of Leakesville, Mississippi, one of my best high school friends and I borrowed Dad's car on Christmas Eve and cruised around town for a while. At some point in the evening, we decided it would be fun to buy some firecrackers and pop them around the neighborhood. In Leakesville, we were allowed to do this as long as we were careful and didn't pop them in mailboxes, which Leakesville residents didn't have anyway.

We purchased about six one-dollar packs of firecrackers (which, back then in 1972, equals six hundred firecrackers total), unraveled them all into a paper grocery bag, and put them on the floorboard of the passenger side so my friend could toss them out his window.

It was cold, probably in the lower thirties, so he kept his window open about two inches. This would allow him to light the firecracker with the lighter stick, and toss the firecrackers out of that little crack in the window and POW!

After we had popped about four or five of them I thought, *"Hey, what if one of those things goes off in the car?"*

We were right at an intersection on the back streets of town and I was making a left turn when all of a sudden, I heard POW. Then POW, POW, POW, POW, POW, POW they went. The whole bag exploded in the car.

Here's what happened in slo-mo, frame by frame. My friend was holding the lighter stick in his hands between his knees. The bag of the remaining 595 firecrackers was on the floorboard between his legs. He accidentally dropped the lighter stick into the bag and it started a chain reaction. I wasn't sure what to do, so I opened my door and rolled out of the car while he was still in the car fighting a losing battle. He should have just left them alone and gotten out of the car. But no, what does he do? He reaches down, grabs the bottom of the bag, and attempts to squeeze the exploding firecrackers through the two-inch crack of the window on his side. All the while these things are exploding at a rapid rate. The sound was unbelievable. Well, since that wasn't working, once again, you'd think, *OK, common sense will kick in here any minute and he'll open his door and get out on his side.* But no, he rolls across the seat and gets out on my side. Remember that I never put the car in park and it's still moving driverless toward the ditch.

After we got over the shock of what had just happened, we got back into the car and drove back to his house. When we opened the door to his bedroom and turned on the light, I couldn't quite put my finger on it, but something wasn't right. My friend's bangs were totally singed and curled backward,

116

and he had no eyelashes or eyebrows. His jacket and shirt had burnt spots and holes all over them. The firecrackers had even popped upward into his bell-bottoms and exploded in his boots, leaving holes in his socks. It was a miracle that either one of us made it out of that ordeal alive.

We eventually laughed about this whole thing. My dad never did. It was HIS car, remember?

UP, UP, AND AWAY

When my husband and I were serving as children's church directors, we scheduled the month of June as Father's Day month. Each Sunday, one of the fathers of our church would come and talk about his work with the children.

One Sunday, Frank Bush, a building contractor, came and showed the kids how to build crosses. Another Sunday, a father who happened to own a generator repair shop brought in a generator to show to the kids, and explained how it worked. My husband, who was an LAPD sergeant at the time, brought a police car the following week. And finally, there was Dan Jenkins. Dan owned his own crane company and had agreed to bring his crane to the church and demonstrate it to the kids.

While Dan was getting the crane into position, I was in the children's church room, serving refreshments. I figured that if the children were going to get a sugar rush from the fruit punch, what better way to burn it off than outside, climbing on the crane.

Some twenty minutes later, I got the signal that Dan was ready. I lined up the children in a single file and we began our trek out to the parking lot. Everyone was behaving relatively well until we rounded the last corner, then the giggling started. The children were laughing and pointing at something, but I didn't know what until I rounded that last corner myself. When I did, I gasped! For there, hoisted about a hundred feet up in the air, was my car! Dan had strapped it onto his crane, and now it was dangling high above the church. When people drove by the church that day, they must have thought we were one church that really took our "No parking in the pastor's parking space" rule very seriously!

PLEASE RELEASE ME
Nicole Franchino, Student

It was the Saturday before Super Bowl XXXIV and I was going to see *Toy Story On Ice* with my friend, Joanna (I call her Jo), her grandmother, mother, and aunt. We live across the street from each other, so we are really close friends.

I went over to Jo's house between 3:45 and 4:00. While I was sitting in the dining room talking to her grandmother, Jo started looking through the drawers in the china closet. She looked at a few stacks of pictures, then pulled out a pair of her grandfather's handcuffs. Putting one cuff on the arm of the chair, she proceeded to play with the other one.

When her grandmother left the room to talk to someone in the kitchen, Jo dared me to put the other handcuff on my wrist, assuring me they were fake. They did appear to be fake, so I did it.

They weren't fake! It was now 4:15 and I couldn't move because I was handcuffed to a chair!

We called out to Jo's grandmother, who quickly came to the rescue but couldn't stop laughing long enough to do anything about it. Jo's grandmother called the landlady, Barbra, but she couldn't stop laughing either. Barbra's husband, James, who stopped by on his way to church, also laughed, but at least he called the police department.

The police department assured him they had an international key to all handcuffs. After I had waited, handcuffed to the chair, for about twenty minutes, the police arrived, but the international key didn't work. Finally, Anthony, who lived upstairs and was also a close friend, came down. He watched while the officer struggled with the lock, then said he had a pair of bolt cutters downstairs if we needed them. Nothing else seemed to be working, so he went and got the bolt cutters. The officer, Jo's grandmother, and Barbra held the skin on my arm down while Anthony cut the handcuff off my wrist. It was now a quarter to five. At five o'clock we went to Egan's Diner, had our dinner, then went on and enjoyed the show.

When we got home I told my parents all about *Toy Story on Ice*, the dinner, and why there had been a police car in front of Jo's house.

"No one can make you feel inferior without your consent."
Eleanor Roosevelt

WHERE'S THAT IN THE SCRIPT?

During a Sunday night performance of a play which I had written and directed, my three-year-old son, Rusty, sat attentively with his father near the front of the church. This particular play featured a living room set (which was my own living room furniture) for one of the scenes.

Shortly after the curtain opened for that scene, revealing

119

our sofa, easy chair, lamps, and various other pieces of furniture from our home, Rusty felt so much at home that he sprang up from his seat, darted down the aisle to the platform, and dove onto the sofa, right in the middle of the performance!

No, it wasn't in the script, but he got the biggest laugh and applause of the evening.

FOLLOW US

When Al Janssen of Focus on the Family came to Nashville, he arranged a meeting and dinner with comedian Torry Martin and myself. We first met at an office here in Nashville, from which Torry and Alaskan radio disc jockey Joe King, in Torry's car, were to follow Al and me, in my car, to the restaurant. En route, I suggested that we play a practical joke on Torry and pull into the most rundown place we could find and pretend that's where Al was planning on taking us. Al agreed, and we soon found the perfect place.

The plan worked great, that is, until Torry didn't see us turn into the driveway of the rundown fast-food eatery. He kept right on going, thinking we were up ahead somewhere. Had he known the name of the real restaurant we were going to, there wouldn't have been a problem. But he didn't. He was just driving, trying his best to "catch up" to us.

Our laughter suddenly turned into sick feelings in the pits of our stomachs. We knew he was looking forward to this nice meal and the opportunity to discuss business. We knew he didn't have a cell phone, and there was no way we could reach him in the car. We knew that he'd probably be so certain we were in front of him that he'd keep driving all the way to North Carolina. And more importantly, we knew we were in big trouble!

We got out of my car and stood on the side of the road, praying, hoping that he'd turn around and retrace his steps. We waved frantically at every black truck that passed by, but none of them were his. At least not for that first hour.

Finally, we saw them. They had turned around and were now pulling into the driveway. Torry had that look of concern, that "Are you guys OK? What happened?" look that only makes you feel worse. Joe stayed in the car to rest (or recuperate), and Torry went in with us to eat.

Yes, into the rundown fast-food place. We stayed there because we didn't have the heart to tell Torry about the practical joke. At least, not until after he'd gotten some nourishment. In fact, waiting until we were in our car with the windows rolled up and the doors locked sounded like a pretty good idea, too.

But we did finally confess. And believe it or not, Torry even laughed about it. He told us that the whole time he was eating he kept thinking, "Boy, I'm gonna call Focus on the Family and make a donation, because if this is all they can afford they're really in trouble!"

You see, that's why I like hanging around with comedians. They can usually see the humor in any situation, and that helps insure me a long life span.

"The most wasted day of all is that during which we have not laughed."

Sebastian R.N. Chamfort

Chapter 12

'TIS BETTER TO GIVE THAN TO RECEIVE

> *Who can discern his errors?*
>
> PSALM 19:12

"To make a mistake is human; to stumble is commonplace; to be able to laugh at yourself is maturity."

William A. Ward

Have you ever received a gift from someone, which you graciously accepted, then had something happen that made them think you didn't like it? Perhaps they were standing in line behind you while you were trying to exchange it at the store or they happened to attend the wedding shower where you gave the rewrapped gift away. But what if you did actually love the gift, but circumstances made it appear embarrassingly otherwise?

IS THAT MY BOOK IN YOUR TRUNK?

One day not long ago, a good friend and fellow author was helping me take some boxes from my office to my car. I handed him my trunk keys, thinking nothing about it, but when he opened the trunk, there was the personally autographed copy of his book which he had given me a month or so before. I know there was a good reason why I hadn't taken it out of my car, but at that moment I couldn't think of it.

I think I was taking it from my work office to put in my home office, but after the three-and-a-half-hour drive home I had forgotten all about it being in my trunk. That theory sounded the most logical, because I really did love his book, but as each word of explanation left my lips, I could feel his suspicion growing. Did I really like the book, or was I saving it for notepaper should I get stranded by the side of the road and need to make an SOS sign? Did I think he had any talent whatsoever, or was this my way of telling him to get a day job?

After numerous attempts, I finally was able to convince him that I indeed did appreciate his work and believe in his talent. That would have been the end of it, had he not then glanced inside my car and noticed another book, which he had given me for a Christmas present tucked safely in a storage area behind the backseat. It was April. We both had a good laugh and I didn't even try getting out of that one.

Thankfully, he knows my heart and forgave me.

NEVER LOOK A GIFT TURKEY IN THE MOUTH

At my house, our motto is "any meal you can walk away from is a success." One dinner disaster, however, outshines all the others.

It was Christmas. Mark Lowry had sent me a smoked turkey for a gift. "The best smoked turkey in the world," he beamed. And it probably was. At least, before I got hold of it.

Now, I'll be the first to admit I'm not the best cook in the world. But I try. For years, I had observed my mother cooking turkey through the night hours, and figured that's what you did. It didn't occur to me that she probably got up and turned off the oven periodically throughout the night. Nor did it occur to me that a "smoked turkey" was already cooked and only needed heating up.

After seventeen hours in a 350-degree oven, I figured the turkey had to be done. The smoked aroma was fantastic and gave no hint as to what condition the turkey was in beneath the aluminum foil wrapping.

Confident I had cooked a masterpiece, I brought the silver-wrapped mound to the table for the traditional unveiling. But when I tore open the foil, that poor turkey looked like some sort of sacrificial bird. Its leg bones were protruding in opposite directions, about four inches beyond the shrunken thigh meat. It was blacker than asphalt, and about as tender. As if I weren't embarrassed enough already, I remembered that one of my dinner guests was a professional chef.

When I told Mark about the incident, he was sick. All that delicious turkey having to be thrown into the trash. He's forgiven me, but now he sends me fruit for Christmas.

PAYDAY

One of the Bob Hope writers got embarrassed when he tried taking a shortcut with his material. The assignment was to write baseball jokes. The writer couldn't see the need for this, since it was an assignment we got every year. "Bob," he said, "we've written hundreds of baseball jokes. Can't you just use some of the old ones from the files?"

Bob said, "I pay you with new money, don't I?"

EMBARRASSING MOMENTS IN HISTORY
(undocumented, of course)

"My fellow physicists, I have discovered something remarkable. E=MC ... E=MC ... Drat! I knew I should have written that down!"

Albert Einstein

"Aw, Mom, come on. None of the other kids at Little League have to wear a stovepipe hat."

Abraham Lincoln

"Mr. Watson, come here, I ... uh ... sorry, wrong number."

Alexander Graham Bell

"But, officer, I didn't know throwing a dollar across the Potomac was considered littering."

George Washington

"I said, 'Charge!' Now, come on. How many Indians could there be?"

General George Custer

"You *had* to make an airplane for our science project, Orville? Now how are we ever going to fit it into our locker?"

Wilbur Wright

PINNED DOWN
Sandra Judd, Editor

A good friend and neighbor, Ross, was celebrating his birthday. An avid and expert cook, he had previously described to our family a very special rolling pin that he had his eye on. A very large and heavy rolling pin. Of course, this is what we chose to give him.

When we arrived at the party, Janet, our hostess, commented on the weight of the gift we had brought, and asked curiously, "What is it?"

"A rolling pin," we told her.

"A rolling pin," she repeated, amused with what she thought was an interesting way to keep the real gift a secret. The box was so big and so heavy, she knew that it could not possibly be what we had said it was.

When the time came for Ross to open the gifts, he held our box carefully in front of him. "I wonder what this could be?" he asked. Happy to join in on our little joke, Janet quickly replied, "It's a rolling pin!" Our eyes bugged noticeably, but Janet just smiled happily.

Needless to say, when the box was opened and the contents were revealed, Janet was mortified. Fortunately, Ross has a good sense of humor, and we were all able to share in the laughter.

Since that time, I and several members of my family have used a rolling pin as our generic guess as to the contents of any package, especially those packages whose shape or size make them most unlikely. This tripped me up, however, at my own wedding, when my sister-in-law proudly presented us with—you guessed it—a rolling pin. I, of course, oblivious to the contents, made my standard declaration: "It's a rolling pin!" My sister-in-law, unaware of our inside joke, couldn't have been more disappointed at the lack of surprise her gift had generated. And me? I keep my guesses to myself now.

OUT OF THE MOUTH OF MOMS
Dave Tippett, Published Award-Winning Playwright
Lillenas Drama Development Team

My fiancée and I asked a good friend to videotape our wedding, back in 1984. Unfortunately, our friend forgot to bring the tripod for his video camera on the big day, so the resulting video is so shaky that I still have to take Dramamine to watch it.

At the time, we didn't complain about the quality of the tape to our friend, as he was doing us a favor and he felt bad enough about being tripod-less that day. However, we did whine about it to other family and friends every chance we got.

At our one-year anniversary, we invited a close group of friends (including the guy who shot it) to watch the video, and met at my parents' home to do so. As we watched the jumpy tape, my mom regaled us all with negative commentary on the quality of the tape. Of course, she had no idea that the guy who had done the taping was sitting right next to her. After ten or twelve comments, my father sneaked out of the room, wrote, "The guy who taped it is sitting next to you," on a napkin, and slipped it to my mom in mid-critique.

She read the napkin, and then decided (in a desperate attempt to save further humiliation) to suddenly switch gears and lavish exotic and gushing praise on the tape ... which, of course, included the line, "Hey, Dave and Jill ... this isn't as bad as you said it was!"

"Happiness exists only in acceptance."

Denis De Rougament

Chapter 13

EMILY POST, WHERE ARE YOU?

Let the words of my mouth, and the meditation of my heart, be acceptable in thy sight, O Lord, my strength, and my redeemer.

PSALM 19:14, KJV

"Allowing an unimportant mistake to pass without comment is a wonderful social grace."

Judith Martin

Manners, or rather the lack of them, can get us into some pretty embarrassing situations. We talk with a mouthful of food and wonder why everyone at the table starts opening their umbrellas. We try to sneak out a silent belch and all of a sudden one is escaping our lips that interferes with NASA transmissions. Or we yell to someone from across a crowded room only to discover it's not the person we thought it was.

Sometimes manners can get us into trouble even when we are using them. We rush to open the door for a young mother carrying an infant, only to have that door swing out and hit the elderly lady on the other side. Or we offer to carry groceries for someone because it appears they can't see where they're going, then accidentally trip over the planter that we didn't see and crack all their eggs.

Manners. Sometimes you just get embarrassed—with or without them.

TIME SURE FLIES ...

When my husband and I first married, his social graces still needed, shall we say, some work. One night we had some friends over for dinner. As risky as that might sound, everything went off without a hitch. They even complimented the food. Well, they didn't actually compliment it, but no one fed it to the house pets.

After dinner, we all retired to the living room, where we spent the next several hours laughing and sharing stories. And more stories. And more stories.

It was starting to get late, and since my husband had to get up early the next morning for work, he decided there wasn't time for subtle hints or discreet yawns. He decided to try a more direct approach. Rising, he simply said, "We're going to bed ... you can let yourself out." I'm happy to say his social graces have improved over the years.

TWO FORKS FOR THE PRICE OF ONE

My mother was a manager and buyer for a well-known department store, and as such, she got invited to attend many formal banquets. My father didn't always feel comfortable at these events and thus attended only a few of them.

At one such banquet, my father happened to notice that his place setting looked a little odd. He had two forks instead of the one he was used to. He waited for the right moment, when there was a lull in the conversation, then, thinking he was being quite helpful, held up his used salad fork and announced sincerely, "I think I've got someone else's fork."

EMBARRASSING MOMENTS FROM THE BIBLE

"Sorry, I didn't mean to come flying into your beach party like this, but well, you see, I've been in the belly of this big fish for three days now, and ... uh, never mind...."

Jonah

"What leaf?... Oh, that leaf. It was all Eve's idea, God. You know women. They're always trying to dress us."

Adam

"I'll go ahead and let the little squirt shoot his slingshot, then he's going down! He's going down!"

Goliath

HUMBLE PIE
Heidi Saxton, Author and Editor

I had this boyfriend once who, for all his other charms, seemed to think I needed cooking lessons. "Here, Heidi. Use this knife. Chop the onion a little finer...." And so on, and so on.

One day I was making a pie crust. My friend stood and watched me until I couldn't stand the quiet any longer. "What's up, Jason?"

"Oh, I've never made a pie before. I was just watching to see how you did it."

I smiled.

The next time Jason came over, I opened the door and found him standing on the front porch, holding the most cookbook-worthy lattice-top blueberry pie I had ever seen. "I brought you this," he said. "Thought I'd try my hand at a little pie-baking." He had picked the blueberries himself that very morning. Terrific.

That night after supper, I went into the kitchen to serve dessert. To my surprise, when I plunged the knife into the pie, it didn't even make a dent. In fact, no matter how many times I hit the pie with the knife, it came bouncing back.

I contemplated my options. *This is too good to waste*, I thought. Carefully I picked up the pie, brought it into the dining room where my family was seated, and set it in front of Jason, along with a stack of serving plates. "I can't bear to cut into this, Jason.... It's too beautiful. Will you do the honors?"

Confidently he picked up the knife, grinned at my parents ... and nearly broke off the knife tip trying to hack his way into dessert. After struggling for several minutes, finally we helped him scrape out some of the blueberries, which is all we could salvage.

I know it wasn't the nice thing to do, but it sure was effective. He never made fun of my cooking again.

"I have often regretted my speech. Never my silence."

Xenocrates

"Success is going from failure to failure without a loss of enthusiasm."

Winston Churchill

Chapter 14

IT COULD HAVE BEEN WORSE

> *The troubles of my heart are enlarged: O bring thou me out of my distresses.*
>
> PSALM 25:17, KJV

"There are no mistakes, no coincidences. All events are blessings given to us to learn from."

Elizabeth Kubler-Ross

There's one ray of hope shining through the cloud of each and every embarrassing moment. No matter how bad that moment was, no matter how red-faced we are or how humiliated we feel, it could always have been worse. It may not look like it at the moment. In fact, we might think nothing else could possibly go wrong. But believe me, more can go wrong. More can always go wrong. Just read about a few of these close calls and consider how thankful the persons involved must be that things didn't get any worse.

WAS THAT A YEA OR A NAY?

One day one of the deacons of a church went to visit the pastor at his home. The pastor's wife answered the door and told the deacon her husband was upstairs cleaning his gun in their bedroom. As she made her way up the staircase to get him, the gun accidentally discharged and the bullet went through the floor, miraculously missing everybody. The pastor apologized profusely and was, of course, forgiven. I'm sure he had a board of six "yes" men after that, too.

CORRECTION NOTICE IN THE DETROIT NEWS

"A map marking the path of Hurricane Elena in yesterday's *News* erroneously placed the state of Oklahoma where Missouri should have been. The hurricane was blowing, but not that hard."

TICKET, PLEASE

There's a medical van driver in Southern California who has got to be laughing to himself about this one.

When my father was recovering from a heart attack, his doctors arranged for him to travel from the hospital to a rehabilitation center for physical therapy. On this one particular day, the medical van driver escorted my father in his wheelchair, into the van and shut the door. What he forgot to do, though, was lock the wheelchair. So, at every stoplight, stop sign, crossing guard, and virtually every other time that van came to a stop, my father would roll all the way to the front of the van. Then, just as Dad would start to knock on the glass divider behind the driver, the driver would take off again, sending my father rolling all the way to the back of the van. This went on for the entire trip! For every mile that van was traveling, my dad was traveling three.

By the time they arrived at the rehabilitation center, my dad had already gotten a good workout. His hair was in his face, his shirt had long since come unbuttoned, and he was just waiting for that driver to open those rear doors. But not so he could give him a piece of his mind. Far from it. When the driver opened the door and realized what he had done, he immediately started apologizing. My dad just smiled and said, "That was better than a ride at Disneyland!"

ON A ROLL

Speaking of runaway wheelchairs, someone once told me the story of an usher who was trying to help a lady in a wheelchair get to the front row of a sloping sanctuary. Somehow the wheelchair got away from him and the lady and wheelchair went flying down the aisle in the middle of the service. The congregation watched with their mouths gaping open as the woman took the ride in stride and simply yelled, "Wheee!" as she rolled all the way to the altar.

AND HOW MUCH FOR MY TRADE-IN?

Once when my husband and I were in the market for a new car, he drove by a dealership and decided to pull in and see what they had to offer. This came on the heels of a week of car shopping, so I was in no hurry to get out of our yellow mini-truck and go through the process all over again. I told him if he found something he liked he could always come back to the truck and get me. I then climbed into the covered bed of the truck for a nap.

My husband did find something he liked and got so far in the negotiation that the salesman wanted to get an estimate on our trade-in by having the used car mechanic test-drive the car. The only problem was, no one told the mechanic that there was a lady sleeping in the covered bed of the truck, and no one told me that I was going for a ride with a complete stranger.

When I woke up several miles down the road, I was surprised and frightened to find a strange man driving me away from the dealership. I thought I was being kidnapped! So I screamed. The mechanic was even more surprised to discover a lady in the bed of the truck, so he screamed. It was like that scene in *E.T.* when E.T. and the youngster both scream at the same time when they first see each other.

After we both calmed down, we explained how we'd each gotten into this predicament, and had a good laugh.

Now, though, when my husband and I go shopping for cars, he's quick to say I don't go with the trade-in. Well, most of the time he does. It's OK, though. My Blue Book value isn't all that much anyway.

DON'T GET UP—IT'S JUST US

While at a conference in Estes Park, Colorado, I went to dinner with friends, John and Linda Styll, publishers of *CCM* magazine, and Bob and Dorothy Baker.

When we returned to the lodge where we were staying, Linda and I were still deep in conversation, and she walked with me to my room so we could finish talking.

Stopping in front of my door, I rummaged through my purse for the key. Finally, I located it (hiding between the half-melted Snickers bar and the tin of Altoids) and inserted it into the keyhole. As I turned the knob and started to push open the door, we heard what sounded like voices inside. It was one of those surreal moments when you talk yourself out of admitting that you're hearing what you think you're hearing.

We didn't think anymore about it and walked on in, still talking and laughing, until we happened to notice several people looking up at us, wide-eyed and quite surprised. There was a lady, too, whom we seemed to have caught in midflight as she was jumping up from her bed and diving for the opening door.

Immediately, questions started rushing into my head. How did this family get into my room? Why were they in my room? Why were they in their pajamas in my room? Was this my room? If it wasn't my room, why did my key open their door? Unfortunately, only questions rushed into my head. The answers didn't want to come anywhere near it. So we did the only thing we could do—we apologized profusely, backed out of the doorway, and laughed all the way back to my real room.

Needless to say, we were embarrassed, and for the rest of the week, we couldn't erase that image of them, with their wide-eyed, open-mouthed looks, from our minds. To this day, I don't know why my key opened their door. But now I always double-check my room number when I go to a hotel. Or at least carry a stack of towels and some tiny bars of soap in my hand, just in case.

STOP THAT CAR!

After dropping my sons off at elementary school one morning, I realized one of them had forgotten to take his lunch money. I quickly jumped out of the car, but since I was going to leave my purse behind, I decided I'd better lock the car. No, I didn't lock my keys inside the car. That would have been too simple. I had the keys right in my hand.

What I did forget, though, was to put the car in park. My locked car was now rolling down the street in front of the school with me chasing after it. Inserting a key into a moving vehicle quickly proved to be no easy trick. I ran alongside the car for the length of the parking lot, passing several driveways before I was finally able to maneuver the key into the lock and open the door. I then jumped inside the moving car and slammed my foot on the brakes—which was good. There's no telling how much detention I would have gotten for driving into the school cafeteria.

WELCOME TO YOUR NEW HOME

A doctor I met once shared this story with me. It seems she had just moved to the town and she hadn't quite become familiar with her new surroundings. So when she went to visit one of her elderly patients who was going to be transferred to the Oakdale Convalescent Home, she inadvertently got its name mixed up with that of the Oak Grove Cemetery.

"Tomorrow you're going to be going to Oak Grove," the doctor said.

"But I don't want to go to Oak Grove," the elderly woman protested.

"I'm sorry, but you have to go to Oak Grove."

"But I don't want to go there," the poor woman continued to plead.

"I'm the doctor, and I'm going to be sending you there in a day and a half!"

Luckily, the doctor realized the confusion before the transfer was made.

"Finish each day and be done with it. You have done what you could; some blunders and absurdities have crept in; forget them as soon as you can. Tomorrow is a new day."

Ralph Waldo Emerson

Chapter 15

BOY, DO I FEEL STUPID

> *In you I trust, O my God. Do not let me be put to shame.*
> **PSALM 25:2**

"Even a clock that is not running is right twice a day."

Polish proverb

Thankfully, a lot of embarrassing moments happen only in our heads, or in front of just one or two people. Privately, we may feel like crawling into a hole, but at least there's not a throng of people cheering us on to do it. Most people aren't even aware that we've had an embarrassing moment. Until they read this book, that is....

A DOG'S LIFE

I pulled into the parking lot of our local post office and parked. I took the letter I needed to mail and exited my car. On my way into the post office, however, I heard someone caterwauling at me from a nearby car. It was that kind of undignified howling some guys make when trying to get a girl to turn and notice them. I tried ignoring it. They say that's the best thing to do. But the more I ignored it, the louder it got. It was so loud now, it was embarrassing. Everyone in the parking lot could hear it. No doubt, people in the next county could hear it. "Rrroooowwwwlllll!!! Rrroooowwwwlllll!" the flirtacious howling continued, growing in intensity.

By the time I reached the door of the post office, I had just about had it with this guy and his unprovoked advances. I normally wouldn't do this, but he had driven me to the point of putting him in his place. I turned around and readied myself to tell him he needed to exhibit better manners. I was going to give him a lesson in the right way to greet people. I was going to teach him the proper way to address a girl. What I saw when I looked in the direction of the sounds, though, made me rethink my speech.

The howling wasn't coming from a rude guy. In fact, it wasn't coming from a guy at all. It was coming from a dog! A very large dog who was loudly voicing his protests about being stuck in a very small car! I felt embarrassed and even thought about going ahead and giving the dog a lesson in manners, but I didn't think someone who drinks out of a toilet would really listen.

RUDE AWAKENING

While staying at a hotel in Northern California, I tried my best to get a good night's sleep. Unfortunately, however, the people in the room next to mine weren't of the same notion. I could hear their television set through my wall until the wee hours of the morning. One o'clock, two o'clock, three o'clock. I couldn't believe the rudeness of those people! Didn't they realize that others in the hotel might like to get some sleep?

Finally, I decided to call the hotel desk clerk to complain. It was almost dawn now and I had been patient long enough. Most people would have complained about such inconsiderate behavior hours before.

But when I reached for the telephone, I happened to notice a clock radio next to it. There were faint sounds coming from it that, oddly enough, sounded an awful lot like the sounds coming from the room next door. When it finally dawned on me, I hung up the phone. The noise that had been keeping me awake all night was coming from the clock radio in my own room!

"If stupidity got us into this mess, then why can't it get us out?"
Will Rogers

THANKS FOR THE HOSPITALITY

A radio disc jockey once shared this story with me. It seems he and his family had decided to surprise some relatives by dropping in on them unannounced. When they got to their house, however, the relatives weren't home. The door was unlocked, so they went on in, waited quite awhile, then went ahead and made themselves some sandwiches.

When they were through eating and their relatives still hadn't shown up, they decided to simply leave a note saying, "Thanks for the sandwiches. Sorry we missed you," and be on their way.

Weeks later, they discovered that their relatives had long since moved from that house.

STUCK ON YOU
Olivia Wolak, Student

It was the end of the school day and I hurried to my locker to get my things. After putting my books into my backpack, I stood up, but something was pulling at my hair. I turned, and to my surprise, I discovered my hair was stuck in the backpack belonging to the boy whose locker was next to mine! He didn't notice at first so he started to walk away. I yelled out his name and he turned around. I tried but couldn't get my hair out of the backpack, and he had a broken arm so he couldn't help much either. Finally, my locker partner came and freed my hair, and me, from this very embarrassing moment.

SAY CHEESE, MR. PRESIDENT

When Bob Hope turned ninety, NBC aired a ninetieth birthday special honoring him. Don Mischner produced the Emmy-winning three-hour special. But when you're a comedy legend like Bob Hope, you get to celebrate your birthday twice. Once for the nation and once at a private party given by your wife, Dolores, for hundreds of your closest friends.

The private ninetieth birthday bash took place in the Hopes' backyard. And what an event it was, complete with a catered dinner under the "big top," clowns, magicians, and a full lineup of entertainers. There were even replicas of the bakery, candy store, and ice cream parlor that Bob used to visit in his childhood in Cleveland. Friends like Jimmy Stewart, Presidents Gerald Ford and Ronald Reagan, Jon Voight, Ceasar Romero, Jane Russell, and a host of other notables showed up to help Bob enter into his tenth decade.

After having the opportunity to visit with former president Gerald Ford for a few minutes, I walked away secretly wishing I'd had the courage to ask him to have his picture taken with me. After all, how many times would I get to be that close to a president of the United States? (Most of them are too busy to come to my Tupperware parties.)

When dinner was announced, my husband and I began making our way to the tent, and somehow ended up right behind Ronald Reagan. I wasn't about to let another president get away.

"Mr. President," I somehow got the words out. "Would you mind having your picture taken with me?"

"Not at all," he said, stopping and turning toward my husband, who already had the camera in place. In my head I was imagining how this picture was going to look on my desk ... framed on my office wall ... repeated in a wallpaper pattern throughout my entire house....

It was dark, so I told my husband to make sure the flash was turned on. Then I posed. Ronald Reagan posed. My husband aimed the camera and snapped.

There was no flash. What had happened to the flash? It was supposed to flash. Suddenly, I felt sick to my stomach. My chance of a lifetime was gone. Or was it?

"You want to try it again?" the president asked.

Again? A president of the United States was giving both me and my camera a reprieve.

"You don't mind?" I asked.

"Of course not," he said. So we posed again. We smiled again. And again, the flash didn't go off. I shouldn't have been surprised. That old camera was in pretty bad shape. The battery cover had fallen off long ago, and we had been keeping it in place with black electrical tape and some chewing gum.

(Don't ask.) I was embarrassed and disappointed, but Mr. Reagan couldn't have been more gracious. I thanked him for his time and let him continue on his way.

I went ahead and developed the film, hoping that by some miracle the picture would turn out anyway. It didn't. It was just a blank negative. Nothing showed up at all. But I had the photo company print out an 8" x 10" enlargement of the shot, and I framed it and hung it on my wall. To everyone else, it looks like a glossy piece of blank paper. But I know it's me and Ronald Reagan!

Some embarrassing moments have some pretty nice pay-offs, though. One night after telling this story in an after-dinner speech, a man walked up to me and asked, "So, did you ever get that picture?"

"No," I laughed. "I had my two chances and I blew it."

"Well, maybe I can help," he said, handing me his business card.

I looked down and read the name on the card—Michael Reagan. I was talking to the former president's son. About a week later, I received a call from Ronald Reagan's office, saying that the president would like to invite me and my entire family to come to his office and have our pictures taken with him!

We went, of course, and Ronald Reagan posed with me alone, with my husband alone, with my husband and me together, and with each one of our three sons alone, then posed for several shots with the whole family together!

I never loved that old camera of mine more!

A WHOLE LOT OF SHAKIN' GOIN' ON
Torry Martin, Comedian

When I first arrived in Alaska, I worked as a camp host for Alaska State Parks. I checked campers in and reminded everyone to put out their fires, to keep their campsites clean, and not to feed caffe lattes to the wildlife.

Have you ever noticed that, no matter how much you warn people, there's always one guy who just won't listen? And from my experience there, it was usually a guy from New York.

People from New York seem to think that just because they can outrun a mugger, they can outrun a bear. But bears don't have the "third strike law." Or Mayor Rudy Giuliani. So there's nothing holding them back.

I remember this one guy. I kept telling him not to leave any food out on the picnic tables overnight, but he just wouldn't listen. So, sure enough, one night a bear came to the campground and went directly to his campsite.

It was about two o'clock in the morning when I heard his screams. Music to my ears. OK, not really music. I wouldn't want a CD of it or anything like that. But I was feeling pretty vindicated.

Evidently, this is what happened. After the bear devoured the leftovers on the table, he headed straight to this guy's camper and started pushing against it. It was as if the bear thought the metal camper was a great big candy machine and all he had to do was shake the snacks out.

The bear actually shredded the aluminum siding of the camper with his claws, which frightened the New York right out of this guy. When I saw him next he was talking like Mel Tillis. "Th..th..th..th..there was a bb..abb.abbear and it shshshhshhook me!"

He still refused to take responsibility for attracting the bear in the first place. "The bears in New York don't act that way," he kept saying.

"Dude, the bears in New York are in a zoo!"

After this incident, it was my duty to go around the campground, posting bear warning signs alerting everyone that there was a bear in the area.

When the Fourth of July came a few weeks later, the campgrounds were packed.

Bears love the Fourth of July. They know with all the campers around they'll get to eat until they get sick. It's our Independence Day—but it's their Indigestion Day. And they know exactly where the food is, from the location of the great big bottle rockets. Those bears just sit up on the hillside and wait for the action to start.

So there I was, sound asleep in my own camper, exhausted from dealing with know-it-all camp visitors, when suddenly my whole camper started to shake. "Bear!"

I leapt up and grabbed some pans as fast as I could and started banging them together. I knew this would distract the bear, but I wasn't sure for how long. So every five minutes I'd bang the pans together, just in case. "Bang! (pause) Bang! (pause) Bang, bang, bang!"

I finally started to relax and doze off. But within minutes, the bear was back! He was really rocking my camper this time, so I started banging the pans again and yelling at the top of my lungs: "Go! Shoo! Get outta here!"

Finally, the rocking stopped. But I stayed up the rest of the night, bug-eyed and banging pans every half hour or so. The next morning I headed out to see if the other campers in the campground had encountered any bears. At the first campsite, I asked, "Did ya sleep OK last night?"

The guy looked at me like I should have known the answer.

"No, not really. But it wasn't the earthquakes that kept me up. It was you banging pans all night."

"Earthquakes?"

"Yeah, two of them. But what the heck were you doing? I mean, I enjoy the Fourth of July, too, but there comes a point when the celebration is over and ya gotta put the pans down, ya know?"

I felt pretty silly, but I covered. "Oh, didn't you know that vibrations from the sound of pans hitting together counters the seismic waves of an earthquake and can, if hit together long and hard enough, keep your camper from being swallowed by the earth?"

He just looked at me.

Tourists.

RED LIGHT, GREEN LIGHT

Some embarrassing moments come simply because we're not paying attention. Like the day I was stopped at a red light, listening to my car radio. The announcer was in the middle of a commercial, so I wasn't really paying much attention to what he was saying. I just wanted the music to come back on so I could get back to enjoying the beautiful day. When the music finally resumed, however, my mind misinterpreted that as the permission I was waiting for to go, so I went. Right through the red light! I didn't realize what I had done until I was all the way through the intersection! I felt pretty stupid and very thankful I hadn't caused a car accident. After all, I would have felt pretty silly having to explain myself to the investigating officer: "But, officer, it had to have been my turn to go! The commercial was over."

WHERE'S THE FIRE?

One wintry afternoon while I was busy preparing dinner, my husband decided to build a fire in the fireplace. Unfortunately, he built it beyond the fireplace. As smoke began filling the living room, he yelled for all of us to clear the house. I still had a saucepan in my hand, and in a panic, ran out of the house with it. Billows of smoke were now following us out the front door, and all the kids and I could do was stand by and wait for him to get the fire out. He did, thank goodness, but I had to laugh when I realized that our neighbors driving by at that moment had to have seen smoke coming out of our house and me standing on our front lawn holding that saucepan.

SHOP 'TIL YOU'RE CAUGHT

I was pretty embarrassed when I came home from shopping one day and found the following message from Bob Hope on my answering machine. He was looking for his writing staff.

"Hello, Martha, this is Bob Hope. Gene's off speaking somewhere, Bob Mills is on the golf course. Si and Freddie have their answering machines on. And you're probably out shopping. Didn't I used to have a career?"

NO TURNING BACK
Ken Bible, Author

This past March, my wife Gloria and I took a tour of the Holy Land with a group from Nazarene Theological Seminary, where Gloria works. Among the sites we visited was Tel Megiddo, the ruins of the ancient city of Megiddo in Israel.

One of the interesting features of the site is a passageway that goes deep underground—many hundreds of steps—before coming back to the surface. During the days of long sieges, this underground passage gave the city access to a water supply that couldn't be cut off during siege.

I have a terrible, irrational fear of heights. When I'm walking downhill on flat, sloping ground, I'm OK, so I thought the descent wouldn't be a problem. But I had just started down when I realized I was in trouble. The descent was a series of very steep staircases, open on each side, which wound hundreds of feet downward. I was petrified and asked if I could go back. But the tour guide told me our bus had already left to meet us at the other end of the passage. There was nothing to go back to. Forward was the only option.

The only way I could force myself to continue was to sit down on my backside and scoot down one step at a time, with a firm grip on both handrails and my eyes glued at the single step immediately in front of me. Men walked behind me and in front of me to help block my vision. The entire time I panted fiercely, like a woman in the final stages of labor.

At long, long last—several agonizing years later, I believe—I made it to the other end of the tunnel, totally wrung out, with the seat of my jeans having taken the beating of their life. Everyone else was already on the bus, waiting. No explanations were asked, none offered.

TAKE YOUR SEAT

One night, my husband and I attended a performance in a nice auditorium. Upon entering the dark and crowded venue (the show had just begun), my husband and I felt our way down the aisle quietly until we came to two empty seats. He took the aisle seat and I tried to take the inner one, but when I went to lower the seat, I didn't feel anything. Naturally, I assumed it was already down and so I sat down.

Unfortunately, the seat wasn't down. It wasn't up. It wasn't there! I went all the way to the cement floor with my popcorn and soda flying everywhere. So much for a quiet entrance.

WHERE'S MY ORDER?
John Mathias, Product Development Manager
Lillenas Publishing Company

One night after my sister received her order in the drive-thru lane of a well-known fast-food restaurant, she looked through the bag and discovered that they didn't have the order right. She went through the line again and tried to tell the clerk over the microphone, but he didn't want to be bothered and kept telling her just to go on. They'd take care of it later. She wanted her food and was going to wait until he gave it to her. He still brushed her off, so she went ahead and drove around to the window. It was then that she discovered why he had been trying to brush her off. They were being robbed.

"Experience is not what happens to you; it's what you do with what happens to you."

Aldous Huxley

Chapter 16

LIVING IT DOWN BY LAUGHING IT UP

> *For he knoweth our frame; he remembereth that we are dust.*
> PSALM 103:14, KJV

"Self-pity in its early stages is as snug as a feather mattress. Only when it hardens does it become uncomfortable."

Maya Angelou

No matter how careful we are, how many precautions we take, how many charm classes we enroll in, we're not going to get through this life without having our share of embarrassing moments. We could memorize every social rule of Emily Post, be a Rhodes scholar or a gifted orator, maybe even receive personal invitations to Buckingham Palace, yet we're still going to mess up from time to time. Embarrassment is an equal opportunity phenomenon. It strikes us all. It doesn't matter if we're male, female, rich, poor, educated, uneducated, white, black, red, yellow, brown, or purple, we're all at risk. It hits people of all faiths, all ages, and all backgrounds. No one is immune.

That rock in the middle of the crosswalk is going to trip whoever comes along and steps on it. It doesn't say, "Wait, that person looks too important to trip. I think I'll wait for the buffoon coming around the corner." If neither one sees it, it's going to trip the VIP and the buffoon alike. And the fact that they tripped doesn't make either one any less important or graceful. It just means there was a rock in the street.

So, don't waste your time wishing for a blunder-free life. There are lots of rocks in the street. You can try your best to avoid them all, to be perfect, but it's not going to happen. At least not in this life. Perfection isn't attainable here. You can thoroughly think through every action, you can plan and train and give it your best possible effort, but you're still going to make some mistakes. That's just the way it is. So go easy on yourself. Everyone deserves a second chance to get something right.

And a third.

And a fourth.

And a three hundredth.

Lighten up. Don't beat yourself up over that sentence you jumbled, that eight-foot pyramid of canned goods you accidentally knocked over at the supermarket, or that wet cement you stepped into. Laugh about it. Apologize if necessary, but forgive yourself as quickly as you forgive others.

Embarrassing moments shouldn't be eternal. They're not the end of the world or of your reputation. Start living them down by laughing it up! And who knows, maybe your moment will be in the next book!

"Fall seven times, stand up eight."

Japanese proverb